WHEN REAGAN
SENT IN
THE MARINES

Also by Patrick J. Sloyan

The Politics of Deception

WHEN REAGAN SENT IN THE MARINES

The Invasion of Lebanon

PATRICK J. SLOYAN

THOMAS DUNNE BOOKS
New York

First published in the United States by Thomas Dunne Books,
an imprint of St. Martin's Publishing Group

www.thomasdunnebooks.com

Library of Congress Cataloging-in-Publication Data

Names: Sloyan, Patrick J., author.
Title: When Reagan sent in the Marines : the Invasion of Lebanon /
    Patrick J. Sloyan.
Description: First edition. | New York : Thomas Dunne Books, 2019. |
    Includes bibliographical references and index.
Identifiers: LCCN 2019024262 | ISBN 9781250113917 (hardcover) |
    ISBN 9781250113924 (ebook)
Subjects: LCSH: United States Marine Compound Bombing, Beirut, Lebanon,
    1983. | Lebanon—History—Israeli intervention, 1982–1985. | United
    States. Marine Corps—History—Arab-Israeli conflict. | United
    States—Foreign relations—Lebanon. | Lebanon—Foreign relations—United
    States. | United Nations—Peacekeeping forces—Lebanon.
Classification: LCC DS87.53 .S63 2019 | DDC 956.9204/4—dc23
LC record available at https://lccn.loc.gov/2019024262

Our books may be purchased in bulk for promotional, educational, or business use.
Please contact your local bookseller or the Macmillan Corporate and Premium Sales
Department at 1-800-221-7945, extension 5442, or by email at
MacmillanSpecialMarkets@macmillan.com.

First Edition: December 2019

10 9 8 7 6 5 4 3 2 1

For Phyllis, the blue-eyed light of my life,
and Nora, Amy, Patrick, John, Conor, Anna, Josephine, Jenny,
Henry, Marion, Joseph VI, Hattie, William, Justin, Julian, and Hana

CONTENTS

WHEN REAGAN
SENT IN
THE MARINES

PROLOGUE

When President Ronald Reagan agreed to support Israel's invasion of Lebanon, he had neither the background nor the foresight to anticipate the river of blood that it would unleash. His disinterest in world affairs made him an easy mark for his unruly secretary of state, Alexander Haig; Israel's obsessed prime minister, Menachem Begin; and its duplicitous minister of defense, Ariel Sharon. Their ambition was to use American military hardware and Israeli troops to change the map of the Mideast. They sucked the unwitting Reagan into a confrontation with ferocious and relentless opponents who conducted diplomacy with knives and bombs. It ended in defeat and blood-spattered humiliation for both Israel and the United States. Surrounded by conflict, ignorance, and incompetence in Washington, Reagan guided US foreign policy to a low point few presidents can match.

Alexander Haig sold Reagan on the Jerusalem government's ambitions primarily as a way to inflict a blow on the Soviet Union's most important client in the Mideast, Syria. In 1981, Reagan was on an anti-Moscow tear, undermining leftist governments in Latin America, Africa, and Afghanistan. He so terrorized the Kremlin that they actually feared Reagan was pushing World War III. Attacking

Lebanon also meant attacking President Hafez al-Assad of Syria, who had 35,000 troops occupying Beirut and Lebanon's Bekaa Valley and was contemplating annexing Lebanon. War with Syria was a certain result of Prime Minister Begin's invasion of Israel's northern neighbor. Along with Defense Minister Sharon, Begin was determined to finish off the Palestine Liberation Organization, which was encamped in southern Lebanon and West Beirut and also got help from Moscow. With Syria out of the way, Begin planned to install a pro-Jerusalem Christian warlord as president of Lebanon. At one point, Reagan secretly approved $10 million for Bashir Gemayel, Begin's handpicked future leader of Lebanon. Israel would have a peace treaty with Lebanon in the north just as it did with Egypt in the south. In the end, however, Gemayel was assassinated and Israel withdrew, leaving Reagan as the rearguard in Beirut.

In some ways, Reagan was a victim of policies of his predecessors and events he understood vaguely if at all. Since the birth of Israel, US policy had supported it at almost every turn of wars with its Arab enemies in 1948, 1967, and 1973. American weapons were supplied to help defend the tiny Jewish nation. Jerusalem's atomic bomb project at Dimona—underwritten primarily by France—had been quietly accepted by every American president since Dwight D. Eisenhower. A landmark in the arming of Israel came after Anwar el-Sadat's surprise attack on Israeli troops during the Yom Kippur War of 1973. The Egyptian president's forces ravaged Israeli armor and warplanes. President Richard Nixon resupplied the country with an astounding $2 billion in new warplanes, tanks, and munitions from American military stocks and factories. Later presidents, and even more often bipartisan US Congresses, gave Israel (as loans that were rarely repaid) squadrons of the world's most advanced supersonic aircraft—F-15 Eagles and F-16 Falcons—and war-fighting electronics.

This multibillion-dollar American arsenal came with Defense and State Department restrictions: None of it could be used for "aggressive" purposes, only defense of Israel. Those prohibitions were effectively waived when Haig, a retired four-star general, gave Begin the green light for the invasion of Lebanon in 1981. When Israeli forces rolled into Lebanon in June of 1982, America's most sophisticated weapons were used to destroy the Syrian air force. In two days, the Israelis piloted Eagles and Falcons and downed at least 86 Soviet-made warplanes. Statements by the White House, State Department, and Pentagon made clear Reagan's support for what Israel called Operation Peace for Galilee. When Sharon's attack stalled against Syrian troops in Lebanon's Bekaa Valley, Israel shifted its focus to the PLO in West Beirut.

For 57 days, Israel pounded West Beirut—the Paris of the Mideast—as horrified television viewers watched, The Arab world was outraged at the United States as well as Israel by the siege of West Beirut. More than ever before, Washington was backing Jerusalem's ruthlessness. American warplanes flown by Israeli pilots destroyed scores of high-rise apartment buildings. Tanks surrounding the city, heavy artillery, and naval gunfire lit the night with explosions. Reagan and his State Department remained silent. It wasn't until Saudia Arabia's King Fahd, brandishing another Arab oil embargo, demanded Reagan halt the siege that the American president intervened.

After the siege, turmoil and chaos in Beirut led Reagan to dispatch US Marines to command a multinational force to stabilize the city. The president was drawn deeper into mountain warfare between Muslims and Christians. When the Marines came under attack, Reagan became enmeshed in battlefield tactics as no other modern president had. He was given a Marine code name—Silver

Screen Six. At one point, he telephoned from the Oval Office to the embattled commander in Beirut, Colonel Timothy Geraghty. Reagan finally ordered the reluctant Geraghty to attack Muslim forces with naval gunfire and warplanes from US ships in Beirut's harbor. Fearing retaliation on his badly exposed Marines, Geraghty refused the air strikes but did unleash naval gunfire.

For the next 19 years after the siege, the United States would suffer the consequences of Islam's revenge. Osama bin Laden said the falling buildings in West Beirut in 1982 inspired his 2001 destruction of the World Trade Center. Even as the siege was under way, Iran's leader, Ayatollah Ruhollah Khomeini, struck back. With permission from Syria, Tehran organized and financed a Shiite militia in Lebanon's Bekaa Valley. Called Hezbollah, the Party of God, militant Muslims from Beirut followed Tehran's orders. Eight months after the siege, on direction from the ayatollahs, Hezbollah destroyed the US embassy in Beirut. Six months after that, they bombed the US Marine headquarters at Beirut International Airport. At the same time, they snatched from the streets American hostages that would continue Reagan's Beirut nightmare for three more years. Reagan's ransom of $50 million worth of US weapons for Iran failed to free the Americans. "We were snookered," Secretary of State George Shultz told the president.

As a reporter for *Newsday,* I covered these events in Washington, Cairo, Jerusalem, and Beirut. Images of some of the 1,600 Palestinian bodies from the Sabra and Shatila massacre are still with me. An American body hanging from the Beirut embassy wreckage made me wince. The corpses of more than 3,000 mainly innocent Muslims killed during the siege littered the streets of West Beirut. Most painful, however, was watching the recovery of 241 US servicemen killed October 23, 1982. Heads, legs, arms, some whole torsos were

scattered everywhere. A massive bomb reduced a 40-foot-tall concrete and steel building to a hole more than eight feet deep full of
concrete slabs and moaning and dying Marines. I knew some of the
dead from interviews. They had made me laugh with their comments and insights.

Not far from the smoking wreckage, I talked to a burly Marine guard full of grief and angry over continued sniper fire from
Muslim forces. The Marine assured me Reagan would strike back.
"The *New Jersey*," he said, "they shoot bullets big as Volkswagens."
The World War II battleship with its 16-inch guns had been lurking
offshore for more than a month. "We're going to give these moth-
erfucking ragheads the whole nine yards." The *New Jersey,* a joke
among naval gunners for its obsolete fire control system, eventually fired into the mountains overlooking Beirut, but only after the
Marines withdrew in defeat and dejection from the city. A Marine
priest who steamed back to their Morehead City, North Carolina,
port with the mauled 24th Marine Amphibious Unit recalled it as
a voyage full of grief. "It was awful," said Captain George W. Puc-
ciarelli.

Reagan refused to strike Iran despite solid evidence of its role in
the embassy and Marine barracks bombings in 1983. Rather than
prolong the conflict and threaten his reelection in 1984, Reagan re-
sorted to his political skills to manipulate perceptions and divert
attention from the Beirut debacle. In the process, he gave a cold
shoulder to the battered Marines there. Instead of accepting his
share of responsibility for the tragedy, he blamed it all on the Marine commander in Beirut. It was his worst moment as commander
in chief. In leaving Iran unpunished, he encouraged the Tehran re-
gime and other enemies to continue their back-alley war against the
United States without fear of reprisal.

To Colonel Geraghty, commander of the slaughtered Marines, Reagan's refusal to retaliate sent a message to Damascus and Tehran.

"Terrorism works," Geraghty said.

1

Four Inches

Fumes from the gas works and lime kilns combined with the slimy flow of the Potomac River to create on certain days a stinky smog along the swampy lowlands of the nation's capital. When the polluting industries were finally removed by 1928, *The Washington Post* declared it was time to drop the neighborhood name, Foggy Bottom, but to no avail. When the State Department moved there in 1947, Foggy Bottom became its nickname—a running smirk at the overdressed Ivy Leaguers who implemented the foreign policy of the United States of America. Long lunches with at least two bottles of decent Bordeaux preceded many directions to Chad or Chile. Career ambassadors around the globe would sometimes snarl about Foggy Bottom as a center of uninformed isolation from the realities of foreign lands.

Full of energy at 50, Henry Alfred Kissinger endeavored to shed this out-of-touch image. The German-born former Harvard professor became President Richard Nixon's secretary of state on Saturday, September 22, 1973. He decided to make his first day on the job Sunday, September 23, when few were around. "Just to see what we had," Kissinger recalled.

On his desk were two new intelligence reports from the day before. "There were Egyptian concentrations near the Suez Canal. And . . . there were Syrian concentrations on the Golan Heights. Being an amateur and not yet a professional, I thought this was rather strange. So I asked the various services what it meant." The reply was terse, blunt, and dismissive.

Nothing. It meant nothing. Just maneuvers.

Instinctively, Kissinger was uneasy about rumblings in the most volatile of all regions now under his purview. Israel was the most important ally of the United States in the Mideast. Egypt and Syria were the most important clients of the Soviet Union in the region. Washington and Moscow had armed and trained the armies of all three. There were simmering confrontations after Israel defeated Egypt and Syria in wars in 1948 and 1967. Any conflict between Arabs and Jews could threaten the world supply of oil from the Persian Gulf and intensify Cold War tensions between Washington and Moscow as they bolstered their client countries. On Monday, Kissinger demanded updates. "And every two days I was told that these were just maneuvers," he said. "The Israelis reported the same thing."

Pressed by Kissinger, the Central Intelligence Agency, the Defense Intelligence Agency, and his department's Bureau of Intelligence and Research came up with a combined conclusion on October 4, 1973:

We continue to believe that an outbreak of major Arab-Israeli hostilities remains unlikely for the immediate future, although the risk of localized fighting has increased slightly as the result of the buildup of Syrian forces in the vicinity of the Golan Heights.

Egyptian exercise activity under way since late September may also contribute to the possibility of incidents.

Two days later, the CIA once more complied with Kissinger's request for an update. A redacted version said:

> Both the Israelis and the Arabs are becoming increasingly concerned about the military activities of the other, although neither side appears to be bent on initiating hostilities. . . . Exercise and alert activities in Egypt are continuing, but elements of the air force and navy appear to be conducting normal training activity. . . . A build-up of tanks and artillery along the Suez Canal, this cannot be confirmed. . . . For Egypt, a military initiative makes little sense at this critical juncture of President Sadat's reorientation of domestic and foreign policies. . . . For the normally cautious Syrian President [Hafez al-Assad], a military adventure now would be suicidal.

When the analysis landed on Kissinger's desk the morning of October 6, Anwar el-Sadat, the president of Egypt, had already launched a war that turned the world upside down. Code-named Operation Full Moon (Operation Badr), it was a two-pronged attack to recover Arab land Israel had seized six years earlier. At the Golan Heights in northern Israel—you can the see the lights of Damascus—Syria sent 1,300 Russian- and British-made tanks against the Israel Defense Forces (IDF) position. In the south, as the minute hand struck 2 p.m. (9 a.m. Washington time) on the west side of the Suez Canal, 4,000 Egyptian cannons erupted in a 53-minute barrage. The first of 40,500 shells—175 per second—landed on the east side of the canal and Israel's massive Bar-Lev

trench line, a World War I–style rampart erected by Chief of General Staff Haim Bar-Lev. For 93 miles along the canal, from the
Mediterranean entrance at Port Said to the town of Suez, there were
20 forts and 35 strongpoints, each with 26 machine-gun bunkers.
Concrete bunkers for troops could withstand a 1,000-pound bomb.
A barrier of concrete-reinforced sand berms reached 82 feet high in
front of minefields, interlocking artillery positions, antitank guns,
and thousands of automatic weapons. Armored brigades of tanks
were staged in support positions. Oil storage containers along the
Bar-Lev fed underground pipes into the canal; once the fuel was
ignited, invaders would face a three-foot wall of fire on the canal,
radiating an incinerating 1,292°F. "One of the best antitank ditches
in the world," Defense Minister Moshe Dayan told Prime Minister
Golda Meir. She and Dayan had poured $300 million ($1.7 billion
today) into the Bar-Lev for the same sort of invulnerability and national pride that France once sought from the Maginot Line.

On the afternoon of October 6, more than 100,000 Egyptian
troops watched 240 Mirage and MiG fighter-bombers streak low
overhead to attack the Bar-Lev, Israeli airfields, and bunkers on the
Sinai Peninsula. In the north, 60 Syrian MiG fighters struck IDF
positions around the Golan Heights. The Muslim troops were given
an extra meal, a dispensation from dawn-to-dusk fasting during
the month of Ramadan; *avoid impure thoughts and evil deeds* is
the admonition of Islam on these holy days. Egyptian frogmen had
plugged the Israeli underwater oil outlets the night before the attack
started. That afternoon, Egyptian commandos slid down the sandy
west bank with rubber boats. On the east bank they rigged rope
ladders for the infantry to scale the Bar-Lev. The night of October 6,
when the moon set and the canal's tide was low, boats with laser-like
water cannons cut away Israel's sand and concrete defensive berms.

Other army engineer craft deployed 10 classic assault bridges—a line of pontoon boats supporting platforms strong enough for 1,250 tanks in the strike force. The bridging locations were picked to outflank the fixed Israeli forts, igloo-shaped redoubts manned by 20 to 30 men. Much of the Bar-Lev shared the same fate as the Maginot Line of World War II—fixed fortresses were simply bypassed. At dawn on October 7, five divisions of Egyptian infantry and armor slammed into the Bar-Lev and five points along the canal. The Egyptian navy performed an amphibious landing, at a sixth assault site just west of Port Said. "It was one of the most memorable water crossings in the annals of warfare," said US Army Colonel Trevor Dupuy, a strategist at the Pentagon for most of his career. With the Bar-Lev a smoking ruin, Sadat's armies surged into the Sinai.

In the Golan, the IDF in Mount Hermon—the mountain range's highest point—oversaw 14 fortified blockhouses that could fire on an array of tank ditches and antitank mounds just inside the Purple Line, the 1967 border imposed on Syria. Minefields and barbed wire were laid to hamper infantry. President Hafez al-Assad wore his uniform on October 6. He had been trained as a jet fighter pilot in the Soviet Union and now commanded 60,000 troops and 1,300 tanks. Israeli forces in the Golan were more prepared for a Syrian attack than their counterparts in the Bar-Lev trench line on the Suez Canal. As a result, Assad's troops made uneven advances on October 6. Yet by the night of October 7, his tanks were in striking distance of the Sea of Galilee and the West Bank of the Jordan.

In Washington on October 7, the intelligence community had no inkling that Egyptian and Syrian armies had overwhelmed Israeli forces. They could only tell Kissinger that fighting was under way.

"Who started this?" Kissinger demanded.

All three intelligence agencies agreed that it must be Israel attacking Egypt. The inbred analysts could only assume the Jewish nation was once more wiping the floor with Arab armies, as it had done in 1948 and again in 1967. As in past failures—Berlin, Cuba, Vietnam—the American intelligence community reported today exactly what they reported yesterday. Intelligence amateur Kissinger ended the briefing.

"I finally said, 'Listen, I'm of Jewish origin. The Israelis do not start wars on Yom Kippur when half of their army is in synagogue.' It took us until the end of the day to put it all together." His displeasure grew after he was presented with maps of the Sinai both vague and dated. "Who in the hell made these maps?" Kissinger was said to have snapped. "Moses?" He, his department, and the Government of the United States were all badly out of touch. Few understood Sadat's real goal, although he had proclaimed it in public two years earlier. War was key for Sadat's plan to achieve peace with Israel. Sadat recounts in his memoir what he used to tell his predecessor, President Gamal Abdel Nasser: "If we could recapture even 4 inches of Sinai territory (by which I meant a foothold, pure and simple), and establish ourselves there so firmly that no power on earth could dislodge us, then the whole situation would change— east, west, all over."

The coordinated October 6 strike by Egypt and Syria so threatened Israel by October 9 that the shaken Jerusalem government unsheathed its nuclear weapons. Fearing a nuclear strike, President Richard Nixon on October 12 yielded to Israel's pleas for a massive resupply of weapons. Warplanes from American units in Europe began arriving in Israel on October 14. From the brink of defeat, a revived Israel crossed the Suez Canal on October 16 in a stunning flanking maneuver that had its tanks poised for an invasion of Cairo. Syrian forces were thrown back in the Golan. A $2 billion resupply of weapons to Israel was announced in Washington on October 19. In Riyadh the next day, King Faisal of Saudi Arabia announced the cutoff of Gulf oil to the United States, Japan, and the Netherlands. The embargo of Arab oil would remain until Israel withdrew from the Sinai, the West Bank, and the Golan Heights, according to the king's edict. On October 24, Israel's counterattack into Egypt alarmed Sadat's supporters in Moscow. Soviet president Leonid Brezhnev threatened insertion of Russian troops unless Sharon's army halted. In Washington, Kissinger alerted US strategic forces to counter the Kremlin's saber rattling. The superpower blustering lasted only a day, but it served to reinforce pressure by Moscow and Washington to end the conflict—just as Sadat had foreseen. A ceasefire was announced October 26.

In 20 days, both Washington and Jerusalem were outwitted and outmaneuvered by Sadat on the tactical Mideast battlefield. With American aid, Israel was able to regain balance on the battlefields in Egypt and outside Damascus.

It took Kissinger longer to comprehend Sadat's strategy of bringing leaders of the Western world to their knees. Within hours of the predictable American rearming of Israel, Arab oil became a bigger weapon than silos filled with hydrogen warheads. King Faisal's embargo on all supplies to the United States, Europe, and Japan would last until Prime Minister Golda Meir returned the West Bank to Jordan, the Sinai to Egypt, and the Golan to Syria. Soon, oil-consuming nations were lining up in favor of the Saudi demands and against Israel. It was also the start of rigged and unrelenting increases in the price of oil that continue to drain family finances to this very day.

At first for most Americans, the Yom Kippur War was another distant fight between Arabs and Jews. This time, the desert war quickly reached deep into America. By November, angry American motorists waited in lines around the block for a rationed 10 gallons of gas. The average price jumped from 38 cents a gallon to 55 cents. The price kept doubling. Soaring inflation caused rising unemployment. The American stock market crashed. A global energy conservation movement was launched. Dealing with energy costs became central to American politics. All US oil exports were halted, a ban that would last until 2017. At least two US presidents went down to defeat caused in part by crushing inflation and double-digit interest rates. American gasoline prices once set by the Texas Railroad Commission were now set by the Organization of the Petroleum Exporting Countries—OPEC. Hundreds of billions of dollars were transferred from the United States and other consuming nations to small Persian Gulf countries once inhabited by nomadic Bedouin tribes.

With the weapon of world oil supplies strapped to his side and newfound respect for Arab armies, Sadat now embarked on a goal first announced two years earlier—a peace treaty with Israel. It was unthinkable. It was impossible. But four years later, Sadat strode into the Knesset to applause from Israel's lawmakers. "I come to you today on solid ground, to shape a new life, to establish peace," Sadat said.

As these earthshaking events unfolded, Kissinger was awed. Before his eyes, this former Egyptian army colonel was transformed into a modern pharaoh who grabbed the Western world by the throat. Kissinger watched as a gambling Sadat dominated the world stage. "A statesman has to take his society from where it is to where it has never been," Kissinger would say years later. "I mention all of these qualities because I met no other leader—and I've known almost all the top leaders of the last 50 years—who exemplified them better than Anwar Sadat." Through war, Sadat would achieve the rarest of gains in the Mideast: peace. Kissinger could not say the same for his own record that year. Kissinger oversaw Nixon's failure to achieve peace in Vietnam—his central campaign pledge in 1968—and implemented the 4,000 secret B-52 bombings of Cambodia and the bombing of civilian centers in North Vietnam. Seeking peace through war, Kissinger spread only death and destruction. Kissinger's only real success was seducing the Washington press corps into promoting his celebrity campaign for the 1973 Nobel Peace Prize for negotiations with Hanoi that went nowhere. Sadat, by contrast, had pulled off in the same year the most audacious strategic initiative Kissinger had ever seen.

"I don't know any expert who, 48 hours before Sadat announced that trip, would have believed that any Arab leader would simply and unilaterally announce himself on a visit to Israel, lay a wreath at the Tomb of the Unknown Soldier, address the Israeli Parliament, and make a breakthrough towards universal peace in the area," Kissinger said years later. "This was a move of extraordinary strength and almost prophetic vision. That is why I call him the greatest man that I have met."

The metamorphosis of Sadat started when he picked D-day to be October 6, 1973, during the most holy time for Muslims and Jews. When he finally had time to reflect, it dawned on Kissinger, as it did on Israeli prime minister Golda Meir, that this man Sadat had achieved an assault of strategic proportions. The start of the Yom Kippur War—the Ramadan War to Arabs—contained the element most sought by any general: surprise. It ranked with George Washington's Christmas attack on British mercenaries in Trenton in 1776 and the Japanese Sunday morning attack on Pearl Harbor in 1941. The Egyptian leader had befuddled Jerusalem's military and intelligence experts with a series of feints from May to August of 1973. Israel limited its mobilization in May to key personnel—not the full-scale alert it would order in August. Moshe Dayan, minister of defense, recalled Sadat's 1973 tactics. "[He] made me do it [mobilize] twice at a cost of $10 million each time," Dayan said. "So when it was the third time round, I thought he wasn't serious. But he tricked me." In August, the Egyptian army, troops, tanks, and missiles, would roll up to the Bar-Lev Line with a threat that forced Israel to mobilize its citizen army. More than 240,000 citizen soldiers raced from their work. Men and women, stockbrokers, sheepherders, kibbutz managers, schoolteachers—all assembled with their IDF infantry, armor, air force, and support units. More than 1,000 Merkava, British Centurion, and American Patton tanks were loaded on lowboy trucks and hauled to tactical locations. Hundreds of fighter-bombers were fueled and loaded with bombs and bullets. And once Israel mobilized, Sadat would simply retreat and send his armies home.

"I had no intention to starting a war [then]," Sadat wrote later. "But as part of my strategic deception plan I launched a mass media campaign, then took various civil defense measures which led the Israelis to believe that war was imminent. In the days when war seemed likely to break out there was full Israeli mobilization, while we enjoyed perfect military calm. I did the same thing in August— and the Israeli reaction was the same."

The feints were part of Sadat's threat of war that he proclaimed in 1971 as necessary to achieve a negotiated return of the Sinai and the reopening of the Suez Canal, which had been blocked since the 1967 war. All he wanted was a foothold on the east bank of the canal to begin negotiations with Israel. By contrast, where Sadat wanted only bargaining leverage, Syrian president Assad wanted only to drive the Jewish nation into the sea. Regaining the Golan was preliminary to sending his tanks roaring through the Israeli city of Tiberias and then the West Bank. Peace with Israel was an unthinkable abomination. Neither Jerusalem nor Washington took these demands of Sadat's seriously. Israel's decision not to mobilize in early October, when Sadat ordered his forces to threaten the Bar Lev line, left only 450 Israeli reservists to defend the 20 forts and 35 strongpoints along the 93-mile long line—probably even fewer, as the IDF soldiers and the entire country observed the Day of Atonement.

Digging more deeply, the October 6, 1973, invasion preceded Sadat's 1972 expulsion of the 30,000 Russian military advisers who had helped rearm Egypt after its devastating losses in 1967. The world viewed the 1972 ejection as a fracture of the Soviet military supply line. But Sadat would write later that the Russians in Cairo were undercutting his threats of war with Israel. Their expulsion gave him maneuvering room and, surprisingly, more and better weapons sooner from the abashed Soviets. Chastened by their expulsion, the Kremlin became pliable. After a Sadat visit to Moscow, the Russian supply line flowed like the Nile at flood stage. That included the latest surface-to-air missiles that would cripple Israel's air force trying to repel Egyptian invaders—the SA-6 Gainful could outrace most planes, even maneuvering at Mach 2.8—more capable T-62 tanks, and countless AT-3 Sagger missiles. The Sagger was a small wire-guided rocket that came in a tin suitcase and was steered to its target by a soldier with a telescope and a joystick. Sadat's disinformation campaign leaked reports that it was too complicated for Egyptian soldiers. But in October, hidden Egyptian soldiers guiding droves of Saggers—sometimes a mile from their target—destroyed hundreds of Israeli tanks. Some clashes left a spiderweb of silvery spent Sagger wires on the desert sand. On both sides, the devastating Sagger became the talk of the battlefield.

In destroying ill-equipped and untrained Arab armies in two previous conflicts, Israel Defense Forces commanders became more than overconfident. As one Israeli colonel put it: "If you come upon a perfectly formed Arab tank battalion on the battlefield, you can be sure of one thing: They are out of gas." That level of contempt for the threat of Arab armies was transferred to the CIA in Langley, Virginia, and the Bureau of Intelligence and Research (INR) at Foggy Bottom. Ray Cline, then undersecretary of state for INR, would later put it this way: "Our difficulty was partly that we were brainwashed by the Israelis, who brainwashed themselves." But the failure of the US intelligence community was monumental. Hours before October 6, the CIA missed a massive evacuation of Soviet citizens from Cairo and Damascus, an alarm bell that more than exercises were under way.

Kissinger would share some of the blame. While Nixon's adviser on national security affairs, he was warned in June by Soviet president Brezhnev that Sadat was serious about an invasion. Sadat reached out to the Nixon White House to explain his intentions months before the 1973 war. A senior Egyptian general met Kissinger secretly in New York to deliver a message from Sadat that ended, "If this discussion succeeds or shows progress, the president will invite you to Cairo." Kissinger slipped a note to a nearby aide. "Do you think it would be offensive if I asked him what the second prize was?" Kissinger wisecracked. He was familiar with Sadat's repeated public statements of a war that could bring peace to the Mideast. "Anwar Sadat made many threats, many statements, none of which, to my shame I must say, I took very seriously," Kissinger said. "Because it was absolutely axiomatic with us that there was no conceivable way that Egypt would dare to start a war." Nixon's national security adviser gave the Egyptian president the American cold shoulder.

Kissinger had underestimated Sadat ever since he had succeeded Nasser, who died of a heart attack in 1970. "I did not understand Anwar Sadat when he first became president," Kissinger recounted. "Our intelligence reports described him as a weak man who had been put into that position because he could represent no conceivable threat. . . . And everyone expected two or three other leaders of Egypt to overthrow him at any moment." In the early hours of the Egyptian invasion, Kissinger dismissed Sadat once more. "For all we knew, [he] was a character out of *Aida*," Kissinger said. It was a reference to Giuseppe Verdi's opera commissioned to mark the opening of the Suez Canal in 1869. The 224-yard-wide waterway's connection of the Mediterranean with the Red Sea and Persian Gulf transformed trade and global politics for more than a century. Cairo sank 15 cargo ships to block the canal entrance after the 1967 defeat.

CIA analysts' missing puzzle piece was an army colonel dedicated to breaking Britain's 74-year grip on the center of Arab culture. Sadat was a career army officer and a fiery revolutionary. His hate for the British colonial government led him to support Nazi Germany (as did Irish nationalists) during World War II. It also cost him almost three years in different prisons. For 18 months, he was held in a Cairo Central cell without a bed, a desk, even a chair. Sadat was the first to secretly organize Egyptian officers who eventually rallied around Colonel Gamal Abdel Nasser in 1952. On the eve of the coup, Nasser gave Sadat the job of ridding Egypt of London's puppet ruler, His Majesty Farouk—by the Grace of God, King of Egypt and the Sudan, Sovereign of Nubia, of Kordofan and of Darfur. There were enough British troops in Egypt to come to the defense of the 300-pound playboy regent. But Nasser's rebel troops surrounded Farouk's stunning Alexandria summer palace, Ras El Tin. Only a few shots were feebly fired by the palace guards, who lacked loyalty.

Sadat signed the ultimatum demanding Farouk's abdication July 26, 1952. In panic, Farouk called American and British diplomats for help. The British chargé in Alexandria showed up in the blazing red and gold uniform of the empire. It was the sort of outfit designed to frighten the natives, Sadat sneered. The chargé stressed Farouk's historical rights and demanded a curfew to protect foreigners.

"Item one," Sadat said, "it has nothing to do with you. It is not a British royal family. As for the protection of foreigners, you should remember this is our country. And from today, nobody should claim responsibility for it except us and us alone." The dramatic demarche was delivered in Sadat's stentorian baritone with a flourish that hinted at his past aspiration to be an actor. Rejection for parts in plays and movies may have been connected with the darkness inherited from his mother, the daughter of a Nubian slave. To one casting director, a young Sadat wrote: "Yes, I am not white but not exactly black either. My blackness is tending to reddish." Within hours of Sadat's performance in 1952, Farouk was aboard his yacht and heading for exile in one of his favorite haunts, Monaco. At the Casino de Monte Carlo he was known for his fondness for oysters—600 in one week—and big baccarat bets. Aboard the warship *Ibrahim,* Sadat watched Farouk sail away. "It was the proudest moment of my life," he later told a biographer.

Sadat was again selected by Nasser, this time to tell the world of the officers' revolt. Sadat's baritone spread the news on Egyptian radio. It outraged London. At 10 Downing Street, Prime Minister Anthony Eden neared hysteria. When his ambassador in Cairo said Nasser could be manipulated, Eden exploded on the telephone. "What's all this nonsense about isolating Nasser or neutralizing him?" Eden shouted into the phone. "I want him murdered, can't you understand? I want him removed. It's either him or us, don't forget that." Along with France, Britain owned the Suez Canal that was a highway to move British goods to India and oil from the Gulf. When Nasser nationalized the canal four years later, Eden went to war. In a secret alliance, Britain and France joined the Israeli invasion of the Sinai and the Canal Zone. For all three nations, it was a fiasco that turned into a debacle. President Dwight D. Eisenhower took up Nasser's anticolonial cause and forced a humiliating retreat for the three invaders. Nasser was hardly grateful. He used American aid to set up a pan-Arab, anti-Washington radio network. Nasser opened the door to Egypt for the Soviet Union. His government was distinctly socialist. Russian engineers took over from Americans the construction of the massive Nile dam at Aswan. During these years, Sadat's military colleagues were elevated above him in rank and power. Most were from wealthy families with important social connections.

Like most born in Egypt over 4,000 years, Sadat started as a *fella,* a peasant. He arrived on Christmas Day in 1918 in the Nile Delta village of Mit Abu al-Kum, where villagers coaxed at least two and sometimes three crops a year. Their alluvial plains were soaked each year with a flooding Nile rich with human and animal waste and other nutrients. Sadat would always claim he was imbued with the village traits of hard work, loyalty, dependability, and common sense. From his Nubian mother, Sit al-Berain, the daughter of a freed African slave, he inherited the Nubian complexion. His father, Mohammed Sadat, worked for a British medical expedition in the Sudan and helped steer his son into the Egyptian army.

After the officers' revolt, Sadat's contemporaries in the army were given senior commands and posts in government. Sadat was sidelined into a public affairs post. Starting with his radio broadcast of the revolution, he became first the voice and later, with television, the face of Nasser's government. He bought tailor-made uniforms for his lean frame. Some officers snickered at his theatrics and uniforms. They nicknamed him "Cardin," as in Pierre Cardin the designer. Even so, he remained articulate, thoughtful, and supportive of Nasser even as Egypt blundered into the 1967 war. When Nasser once again closed the Straits of Tiran and Israel's access to the Red Sea, Jerusalem preemptively launched its most devastating attack on the Arab world thus far. Egypt's Russian-made air force was destroyed, along with most of its armor and artillery. The IDF occupied the Sinai Peninsula to the edge of the Suez Canal. Jordan lost the holy sites of East Jerusalem and the West Bank of the Jordan River. Syria lost the Golan Heights and a section of the Mount Hermon range that borders northern Israel as well as Syria and Lebanon. The loss led to army grumbling and rumors of Nasser's overthrow. Two days before leaving for an Arab summit in Morocco, Nasser called Sadat aside. Nasser feared a coup or worse, and he didn't want to leave a political vacuum. Sadat agreed to be sworn in as vice president. Ten months later Nasser, 52, was dead from a heart attack. Although Sadat assumed the presidency of Egypt on September 28, 1970, his real debut on the world stage came on October 6, 1973.

Kissinger's intelligence community could not see what the Egyptian army was doing at the start of the Yom Kippur War. The Keyhole satellites of today's National Reconnaissance Office (NRO) orbit on an adjustable course, their cameras seeing clearly through night and clouds to instantly relay amazing real-time images to secure displays. In 1973, the NRO's Corona program had to launch a camera satellite on a specific orbit, then eject the film on a parachute that was snared midair by an Air Force transport or from a capsule plucked from the sea. The satellite launches were delayed during the first weeks of Yom Kippur. The CIA finally ordered the Air Force's Mach 3 reconnaissance ramjet, the SR-71 Blackbird, but Britain and West Germany, two of the most important US allies in NATO, refused operating bases for the plane. Fear of angering Arab oil sources was part of the equation. As a result, the SR-71 began surveying the Sinai battlefield from Griffiss Air Force Base at Rome, New York. Blackbird pilot Jim Shelton refueled from tankers six times during the 11-hour flight. Shelton wanted to be over the target between 11 a.m. and noon. "This allows you to have some shadows so the photo interpreters can go ahead and judge elevation," Shelton said. He was concerned about a potential new Soviet surface-to-air missile (SAM). "Russia was developing the SA-5," Shelton recalled, "which was a missile that would go up well above you and then come back down at you." But the Blackbird roared in at more than 2,000 miles an hour at 80,000 feet above the Sinai battlefield. When the Egyptians were ready to fire, the plane was already in Israel. "When we rolled in on the first pass over Israel, my defensive system just lighted up like a pinball machine," said Reg Blackwell, monitoring the electronics in the backseat. Israel, unaware of the secret US spy mission, fired a barrage of rockets. Blackbird projected an electronic image some distance from the plane that sent SAM warheads searching for a phantom target. It was a bit of electronic wizardry that would make scores of US Air Force B-52s immune from Soviet SAMs fired by North Vietnam. The SR-71's Operation

Giant Reach on October 12 finally provided photographic proof of Sadat's Operation Full Moon.

The damage which the Egyptians had inflicted on the Israelis on the Bar-Lev Line and beyond was substantial, reported Dino A. Brugioni of the CIA's National Photographic Interpretation Center. "Most of the fortified positions had been destroyed. It was also obvious that the Egyptians had used flame-throwers for many of the command and living bunkers had been burned. The Egyptians had crossed the Canal in five places. Egyptian assault boats were seen all along the Canal. Rope ladders and ropes could be seen on top of the sand barriers. Craters from aerial bombardments and artillery fire had literally torn great holes in the fortified positions. And 90 Israeli tanks stationed behind the Bar-Lev Line had come forward to be met by Egyptian soldiers firing Russian supplied Sagger wire-guided missiles along with rocket propelled grenades." Brugioni's analysis indicated that most if not all of the tanks had been destroyed. Of the 441 soldiers manning the Bar-Lev, 126 were killed, 161 were taken prisoner, and 154 retreated to safety.

Soviet surface-to-air missiles were deployed along with advancing Egyptian infantry. Israeli pilots were unable to elude the most advanced SAMs, the Russian SA-6. "The SA-6s were wreaking havoc on the Israeli Air Force," Brugioni said. "By Tuesday October 9, the Israelis had reported that they had lost 49 aircraft, including 14 [American-made] Phantoms primarily from the SA-6." With the Bar-Lev a smoking ruin, two Egyptian armies surged into the Sinai and took up defensive positions. Israel launched a major counterattack. The Blackbird had spotted the largest tank battle since World War II. "A major tank battle had begun," Brugioni reported. "Over 1,600 Israeli and Egyptian tanks were involved and the fighting ranged over a large area. We could easily identify the battle lines since the Israeli tank forces consisted of Super Shermans, Pattons, AMX, and Centurion Tanks. The Egyptians possessed Soviet tanks." Israel's counterattack failed. In the Golan Heights, Syrian tanks and infantry dislodged Israeli defenders. Israeli jets sent to attack the Syrian armor were destroyed by the Russian SA-6s. Sadat got more than four inches.

In Jerusalem, Dayan and other generals realized that the Israeli air force alone was not, as previously predicted, enough to repel Sadat's forces. Egyptian and Syrian use of SA-6 rockets had neutralized Israeli warplanes. On the ground, battalions of Israeli tanks were hurled into a counterattack. The roar and clank of the American-made Patton tanks had once been enough to make Arab soldiers flee, but Egyptian infantry and their Saggers picked off 200 Israeli tanks in the first 24 hours. Dayan's counterattack failed to repel Sadat's stand in the Sinai. Within days, 500 tanks, or a third of Israel's armor, were blackened hulks in the desert. Jerusalem was shaken. So were IDF troops used to easy triumphs over Arab armies. "It was a generation that had never lost," said Major General Ariel Sharon. "Now they were in a state of shock. . . . How was it that [Egyptians] were moving forward and we were defeated?" Just as frightening were Syria's initial gains in the Golan Heights, which Israel had seized from Damascus in the 1967 war. Syrian troops and tanks overwhelmed Israeli defenders and threatened Israel's northern border. Defense Minister Dayan redirected warplanes from Egyptian to Syrian targets in the Golan. No one was more rattled than Dayan. In briefing Prime Minister Meir, he harked back to dire moments in history when the Babylonians destroyed Israel's First Temple in 588 BC and the Romans burned the Second Temple 400 years later. "This is the end of the Third Temple," Dayan told Meir of attacks on the north and south of tiny Israel. Dayan, the one-eyed hero of the 1967 war, feared the worst in those early days of the Yom Kippur conflict. At a background briefing with Israeli newspaper editors, Dayan's pessimism caused one of them to burst into tears. Another called Meir to keep the despairing Dayan from speaking to the nation on television. Three millions Israelis were running out of war stocks, and 70 million Arabs had soldiers and tanks to spare.

One measure of the Jerusalem government's desperation was spotted by the SR-71 Blackbird's sweep over the battleground and Israel on October 12. "We were seeing activity at the Jericho missile base," Brugioni said, describing pictures forwarded to the CIA. Despite official denials by the American and Israeli governments, the CIA had been aware of Israel's nuclear weapons program since Eisenhower was president. "We had seen the Israeli development of the Jericho missiles, and the CIA had given the Israelis credit for having nuclear weapons," Brugioni said. Various accounts had up to 12 of the short-range ballistic missiles armed with nuclear warheads put on alert at Sdot Micha Airbase. An additional F-4 Phantom fighter-bomber was also armed with an atomic bomb at Tel Nof Airbase.

As events turned grim in the Sinai and the Golan Heights in the first week of the war, Prime Minister Meir's cabinet considered using one warhead—not as a weapon against the Arabs but as a demonstration. Defense Minister Dayan proposed creating a fireball and mushroom cloud over a remote desert location as a warning. Meir and other cabinet members quickly rejected the proposal. More effective was Israel's display of armed Jerichos for the high-flying Blackbird spy plane. The most comprehensive account was put forward by Seymour Hersh in his 1991 book *The Samson Option*. Hersh had the Israeli ambassador in Washington demanding US rearmament—or Jerusalem would resort to nuclear warheads. But Brugioni at the CIA photo center was one of only two US officials to confirm the preparation of the Jerichos. The other was William Quandt, Kissinger's deputy on the White House National Security Council (NSC). In a review of Hersh's book, Quandt confirmed some key controversial facts and added this: "We did know around this time that Israel had placed its Jericho missiles on alert. It was also conceivable that the nuclear threat might be made if Egyptian troops broke through at [Sinai] passes. This situation, by itself, created a kind of blackmail potential—Help us or else."

In Washington, Secretary of State Kissinger was increasingly wielding presidential power. The presidency itself was denied to him by the Constitution's insistence on only US-born candidates, but he retained control of the NSC at the White House. Nixon was at his Florida home in Key Biscayne, in a haze of alcohol and pills. The painkillers eased the bite of Special Watergate Prosecutor Archibald Cox. With every front-page story, Cox inched closer to seizing White House tape recordings. They would prove Nixon sought to obstruct the investigation of the burglary of Democratic National Headquarters at the Watergate hotel complex.

One instance of Kissinger's authority involved 10 Downing Street calling to set up a phone call in 15 minutes between Nixon and Prime Minister Edward Heath. Kissinger said no.

"When I talked to the president he was loaded," Kissinger said.

Yet Nixon emerged sober for a crucial meeting that would gouge American family budgets for the next 45 years. With Blackbird photos of Jericho rockets on the launchpad, Kissinger and Nixon gave in to Israeli pleas for US weapons. The decision was blocked by James Schlesinger, the six-foot-four secretary of defense who controlled American war stocks. Schlesinger was so convinced Watergate had addled Nixon's judgment that he would sleep on a cot in his Pentagon office so he could intercept any Nixon orders to use nuclear weapons. Alexander Haig, who had risen from Kissinger's military aide to White House chief of staff, recounted the confrontation between the president and his defense chief. It was in the Oval Office on October 12. An economist by trade, Schlesinger feared rearming Israel would cripple the United States.

"Schlesinger had his own policy priorities," Haig recounted, and was concerned that US intervention "on the scale mandated by the president would alienate the Arab nations and might lead to an oil embargo against the West." Nixon staged an angry confrontation with his defense chief. "Now get the hell out of here and get the job done," Nixon said in brushing aside Schlesinger's warnings.

At a cost of $2 billion, Nixon launched Operation Nickel Grass. More than 22,000 tons of jet aircraft, tanks, ammunition, and other matériel was airlifted to Israeli bases. Some American warplanes were flown directly from their plants in the United States. Other aircraft were taken from active-duty US forces in Europe. Eventually, 33,000 tons of military supplies arrived by ship. Israeli soldiers drove the US tanks directly onto the battlefield. Every 15 minutes, a US Air Force C-5A, C-140, or C-130 landed at Israeli airfields.

Operation Nickel Grass set the stage for phase two of Sadat's Operation Full Moon. The American rearming of Israel was just what Sadat had predicted in his war council with King Faisal in 1972. Faisal had a religious bent. He was the first Saudi king to revive the title of Custodian of the Two Holy Mosques, assuming the role of caretaker of Mecca and Medina, Islam's holy cities. At the same time, Faisal harbored hatred for Israel and the Soviet Union.

To him, both countries were identical in political culture and immorality. Faisal agreed with Sadat's plan to turn Arab oil into a weapon. Ahmed Zaki al-Yamani, the Saudi oil minister, made clear King Faisal planned to use oil as a political weapon after discussions with Sadat. All future American appeals to King Faisal were referred directly to Sadat. "We knew that a war was coming," Yamani said in outlining the embargo.

With announcement of the oil embargo, Sadat wanted a cease-fire. The American secretary of state negotiated it. "I received a message very early in the conflict from President Sadat saying that he wanted to negotiate eventually," Kissinger recalled. "And I sent him a message which said, in effect, you can make war with Soviet arms, but you have to make peace with American diplomacy."

Around October 23, the Egyptian 3rd Army was still threatened by General Ariel Sharon's drive into Suez. American rearmament of Israel was in full swing. Sadat was unflappable. "Almost the first thing he said to me," Kissinger recalled, "was 'This is a psychological problem; this is not a political problem. And you have to help me to bring about a change in psychology.'" At the same time, the Soviet Union was resupplying Egyptian forces. As Sharon's divisions cut off water, food, and ammunition supplies to the surrounded Egyptian army, Moscow responded to Cairo's dilemma. From the Kremlin, Brezhnev fired a warning in a letter to Nixon: It might become necessary for Soviet forces to intervene in Egypt's behalf. The threat of Soviet interference on the ground produced a crisis session at the White House—without the president. "I've heard that President Nixon was upstairs drunk," said Ray Cline, Kissinger's expert on intelligence. Four days earlier, there had been a flood of impeachment resolutions in Congress after Nixon demanded Watergate prosecutor Cox be fired on October 20. Nixon had taken to his bed. Haig, his chief of staff, tried but failed to wake him for the Washington Special Action Group meeting downstairs on October 24. Assuming control once again, Kissinger ordered an increase in the nation's defenses as a reply to the Soviet letter. DEFCON (defense condition) 4, then code-named Double Take, was increased to DEFCON 3, Round House. DEFCON 4 called for increased intelligence; DEFCON 3 ordered increased force readiness, although it barely changed actual force deployment compared to President John F. Kennedy's move to DEFCON 2—Fast Pace, the last step before nuclear war—during the 1962 Cuban Missile Crisis. To the world, however, DEFCON 3 may have bolstered Nixon's fast-fading image. Even though he was out of it in bed, Nixon got credit for strong-arming the Kremlin. According to the Soviet ambassador to Washington, Anatoly Dobrynin, Kissinger later assured him that the move to DEFCON 3 was primarily for "domestic reasons." In any event, the superpower bluster vanished quickly.

A dicey cease-fire—gunfire was exchanged by both sides—was replaced October 26 by generals on both sides meeting at Kilometer 101—the exact distance from Cairo on the seaside highway in the Sinai. Those talks evolved into the foundation for Sadat's peace initiative with Israel. While the war in the desert was winding down, the pain was picking up in the United States. The oil embargo induced panic among American drivers and real shortages at neighborhood filling stations. Lines formed around the block. Fill-ups were limited to 10 gallons. Gas stations, increasing the average price from 38 cents to 55 cents a gallon, agreed to a federal plea to shut down on Saturday nights and Sundays. Pump prices doubled and doubled again. Christmas road trips to Grandma's house were canceled.

Sadat's oil weapon struck the freeways near La Casa Pacifica, President Nixon's oceanside villa near San Clemente. California State Police organized rolling blockades on roads built for speed. The 75 mph freeways were suddenly limited to 50 mph. Nixon had been born and bred in California, where Rule 1 was "Don't come between a driver and his car." But pills and whiskey now made him immune to the national turmoil. In the midst of the Yom Kippur War, he had ordered the firing of Special Watergate prosecutor Cox. The grossness of the move cost him his attorney general and deputy attorney general, who resigned rather than fire Cox and undercut the rule of law. To many in Washington, Nixon was, as UPI reporter Helen Thomas put it, a "dead man walking."

Kissinger once again stepped in and conducted almost daily crisis sessions with oil experts and the oil industry on the crippling effects of shortages. Turmoil at every neighborhood gas station and soaring prices demanded political leadership and some sort of relief. Kissinger did not have a clue. At times, he was mystified.

"I don't know what the answer is. I don't even know what the problem is," he said at one meeting. "When people tell me we are consuming six million barrels a day, they might just as well say fifty thousand Coke bottles worth of oil. I don't know what that means. I have no ideas. All I know is when the Prime Minister of Britain says he wants to send somebody over here to discuss the oil situation with one of us and I ask around the Department 'What are we going to tell him?'—or we go up to Canada and I ask 'What are we going to discuss?' and I am told we are just going to discuss—and every other department takes the same position. Interior Department hasn't got a clue. Everyone agrees that if we can get more supply in this country, or cut down the demand—that this will improve the basic situation. That is clear. What I want to know is what the hell we are going to discuss in these negotiations. What do I discuss with these oil men this afternoon? I don't know the answer to this. How do we get at this problem?"

Trying to woo King Faisal, Kissinger's strong suit, became impossible. Faisal learned Saudi revenues would increase with rising prices—from $2 a barrel to $10—even as production and exports were cut back. In diplomatic talks, Faisal would blame Arab radicals for the shortages and the price increases. But it soon became clear that the frail and religious king was the real radical, dismissing pleas from his own pro-Western princes to ease up. As diplomacy failed, frustrations grew. "It is ridiculous that the civilized world is held up by eight million savages," Kissinger said during a November 29 meeting with Defense Secretary Schlesinger. At one point, Schlesinger and Admiral Thomas Moorer, chairman of the Joint Chiefs, proposed seizing oil sources with US Marine invasions of some Gulf States.

The embargo was finally lifted after four months, in March 1974. But the havoc continued. Throughout the crisis, Kissinger assured Nixon that Sadat was working to ease tensions. "He's pro-Western," Kissinger said. The Egyptian president was establishing his role as America's only real hope of tempering the oil squeeze. Kissinger's admiration only grew. From his cross-canal surprise to engineering the oil embargo, Sadat was dominating the world stage. It was the sort of successful diplomatic strategy that eluded Kissinger while at the White House and State Department. He became close with Sadat during Mideast peace shuttles. They were together at Sadat's winter home in Aswan in 1974 when the Jerusalem government finally approved the Kilometer 101 agreement—officially ending the Yom Kippur War.

Kissinger recalled an aide bringing the news in a note. Sadat began reading. "He had tears in his eyes," Kissinger said. "He came over to me, kissed me on both cheeks, and said, 'I will now take off my uniform and I will never again wear it—except on ceremonial occasions.'"

2

Legacy

The Hero of the Crossing glittered in a new uniform. Gold braid was everywhere from the brim of a peaked hat to sleeves and epaulettes on a navy blue tunic with red piping. A green silk sash with gold stars across the chest of Anwar el-Sadat still left room for rows of gold and jeweled medals. The president of Egypt was resplendent. October 6, 1981, was the eighth anniversary of Operation Full Moon. The invitation-only crowd cheered as he stepped from a Cadillac convertible limousine. His backdrop was the soaring modern take on the pyramids of Giza that was the Tomb of the Unknown who died in 1973 driving Israel's armies from the Suez Canal and the Sinai Peninsula. His arrival at the Nasser City parade ground in suburban Cairo was a signal to start the music and marching for a splendid display of Egyptian military power, from screaming jet fighters to the clopping Camel Brigade. Cheers went up for the Lancers on their prancing gray Arabians. Sadat set down his pipe and rose again and again to take the salute from troops strutting before a crowd of generals, diplomats, military attachés, and credentialed dignitaries. Paratroopers landed inside circled targets and then rushed to salute Sadat. The acrobatic air show unnerved the American ambassador, Alfred Atherton. Low-flying jets roared straight for the reviewing stand before pulling up sharply at the last moment.

"I suddenly found myself thinking, 'You know, what if somebody really wanted to wipe out the president, his whole government, and anybody else? If they had that mission and decided to do it, we would be perfect targets,'" Atherton said later. He knew opposition to Sadat's rule was serious. Sadat's peace treaty with Israel made him an apostate, an outcast among Arab leaders. Islamic extremists were plotting his overthrow. Sadat had badly miscalculated three years earlier in accepting advice—and money—from the World Bank. Following orders to modernize the 4,000-year-old economy, Sadat eliminated government subsidies on flour, rice, and cooking oil. Riots erupted everywhere. "Hero of the Crossing, where is our breakfast?" was a favorite mob chant. At least 79 were killed and 550 injured after he called out the army. Sadat finally restored the subsidies. Meanwhile, as an architect of peace between Arab and Jew, Sadat became a celebrity in the Western world. In Savile Row suits and Jermyn Street shoes, he entertained *60 Minutes,* Frank Sinatra, and a steady stream of world leaders. His teen bride—she was 15 and he was 30 at their wedding—had Western ways as well; Jehan Sadat, the daughter of a British mother, rarely covered her hair in public. For his perceived offenses against Islam, Sadat had been dealing with the Muslim Brotherhood for almost 30 years. These bearded men were among more than 1,500 arrested by police in recent months. Sadat refused to listen to security advisers. He proclaimed himself father of sometimes rambunctious children.

Sadat rose once again to take the salute of soldiers who halted a truck pulling an artillery piece. Associated Press photographer Bill Foley said it was just after 1 p.m. "All hell broke loose," Foley said. Four men jumped from the truck and began throwing something. A Russian-made hand grenade bounced off the head of the Egyptian minister of defense, who was sitting next to Sadat, but did not explode. Three more grenades landed, and two exploded. One tore Sadat's new uniform and torso with shrapnel. He fell to the floor behind the marble front of the reviewing stand. The defense minister, General Abdel Halim Abu Ghazala, watched as four soldiers advanced firing automatic weapons. The assassination team leader, lst Lieutenant Khaled Ahmed Islambouly, trained his Swedish-made Carl Gustav machine gun on the fallen Sadat. ABC cameraman Fabrice Mossus ran to the reviewing stand. Islambouly turned his gun toward Mossus, paused after recognizing the desired camera coverage, and resumed firing on the infidels. Two bullets struck Sadat in the chest; one hit him in the temple; one lodged in his neck, one in his right arm, and two above the knee of his left leg. The other assassins hosed the reviewing stand, killing eight and wounding 40. Ambassador Atherton crashed to the floor along with other VIPs. Folding chairs suddenly became snares for escapees. Blood began to pool. Jehan Sadat joined in the screaming. Stunned bodyguards lifted Sadat's bleeding body into his convertible limousine and then loaded him into an army helicopter. Sadat was dead on arrival at Maadi Military Hospital. He was 62 years old.

Two days later, the world assembled to mourn and pay homage to the fallen leader of the greatest Arab nation. Three former American presidents, one king, an array of princes, and political leaders of Europe, Asia, and Africa filled Cairo hotels and guest houses. Getting the most attention on arrival was Menachem Begin. The prime minister of Israel was splashed over Cairo's front pages embracing Sadat's successor, Hosni Mubarak. The former Jewish enemy was now bound by peace treaty to his former Arab foe. Begin owed his political success to Sadat. Operation Full Moon left 2,812 Israeli soldiers dead, a toll that was a sword through the heart of the Jewish nation. Two months later, voters showed their outrage. Begin and Ariel Sharon, by then a reserve general, won 39 seats in the Israeli parliament, the Knesset. Their new party, the conservative Likud, was within a handful of seats of taking control of the government from the liberal Labor Alignment that had dominated since Israel's birth in 1948. For Labor, and Prime Minister Golda Meir, it only got worse. A national commission headed by Chief Justice Shimon Agranat found Sadat's stunning surprise invasion was the result of incompetence and complacency by the Meir government. An interim report on April 1, 1974, called for dismissal of senior military leaders. Thousands took to the streets of Jerusalem and Tel Aviv. Prime Minister Meir resigned nine days later, on April 10. Meir and her party were Ashkenazis, Jews who had fled France, Germany, and Eastern Europe during Adolf Hitler's Nazi reign of terror. She was born in Russia, but her formative years were in Milwaukee, Wisconsin. Her supporters were largely white, well-educated families dedicated to an Israel for all, secular and not dominated by the Jewish religion. Begin, too, had roots in Eastern Europe. He was five-foot-six, with Coke-bottle eyeglasses and thinning hair pasted straight back to his balding skull. With women he displayed the manners of Polish nobility, bowing low and sweeping up their hand for a kiss. In reality, he had been a leather-tough fighter in Jewish self-defense movements since college in Warsaw. When he spoke, followers roared. In British-controlled Palestine, Begin became famous as the bantam leader of the extremist underground, the Irgun. His bombing of the King David Hotel in Jerusalem—91 people were killed—was a landmark in the fight to oust the British government.

Accompanying Begin in Cairo was Sharon, his new minister of defense, a celebrated field commander is Israel's wars, a man Begin referred to as *"mon general."* Sharon was a sabra, a Palestine-born son of immigrant farmers. Thanks to Sadat, Sharon now oversaw one of the world's most potent and technically sophisticated armies. President Richard Nixon's massive $2 billion rearmament of Israel's exhausted war stocks in 1973 was just the beginning. Presidents Gerald Ford, Jimmy Carter, and Ronald Reagan, Israel's supporters in the US Congress continued to grant Jerusalem the best American weapons. That included squadrons of F-15 Eagles, the most advanced interceptor in the world, and the F-16 Falcon. By 1981, Israel had a supersonic air force with the world's most sophisticated radars and air-to-air missiles. Included was the E-2 Hawkeye, the US Navy version of airborne warning and control. Flying a racetrack pattern to the side of the aerial battlefield, Hawkeye used radar and infrared to spot enemy attackers at a great distance. Interceptors were then guided unerringly to the exact launch point for their missiles. Secretly, the United States supplied arrays of electronic battlefield systems that performed astounding feats against surface-to-air missiles—SAMs. Sadat's use of Soviet-made SAMs, most notably the SA-6 Gainful, changed the face of air warfare for the United States as well as Israel. No matter how skilled, many Israeli pilots in US and French jets could not escape the Mach 2.8 SA-6 and its maneuvering warhead. Israeli losses during the Yom Kippur War gave birth to the radar-evading stealth designs for future US fighters and bombers. In the meantime, electronics were deployed that created false images and other decoys on enemy missile radars, duping SAMs.

For Israel, the new arsenal came with all sorts of American-imposed restrictions that were amplified by the Department of Defense and the State Department. Essentially, Israel could use these weapons for defensive purposes only. Begin and Sharon showed up for Sadat's funeral with some plans to use the new hardware resulting from Operation Full Moon offensively. Five months earlier, they had ordered six F-15s and eight F-16s to destroy Iraq's nuclear reactor at Osiraq. To protest the violation of the US ban on offensive use of the aircraft, President Reagan delayed shipments of additional F-16s, but only briefly. Begin and Sharon had even more ambitious plans for Syria when they arrived in Cairo. First word of their strategy began to circulate on Saturday, October 10, on the very spot where Sadat was assassinated four days earlier. The Nasser City parade ground had been selected as the assembly point for a cortege of notables to follow Sadat's coffin on a horse-drawn caisson. His casket would be placed in a marble vault at the base of the Tomb of the Unknown.

Journalists were directed to a building where the cortege would form. It also served as the makeshift tomb of the shah of Iran, who had died a year earlier, and I inspected the small corner that held his casket. American support for the shah in his final years helped fuel the religious revolution in Tehran. Ayatollah Ruhollah Khomeni would urge his followers to ransack the US embassy and take American diplomats hostage.

Wandering into the next room brought back a flood of memories. There was Richard Nixon. It was the first time I had seen him since August 9, 1974, when he walked by me on the South Lawn of the White House and waved good-bye to his presidency as he boarded Marine One.

In the holding room, glued to his side with his mouth in Nixon's

ear, was Secretary of State Alexander Haig. To one side was Haig's
wife, Pat. On that day of Nixon's resignation seven years earlier,
Haig was his chief of staff. During an East Wing reception, I asked
Haig how Nixon was holding up. "He's serene," Haig said. *A serene
wreck,* I thought. Now, Nixon was brown with a tan and beaming as he walked toward me. He was a robust 68. I was one of
thousands he knew personally. His politician's trick was to associate
your name with your college mascot. With me, it was Maryland's
terrapin. I had covered him since his 1968 campaign plane until his
last moments on the South Lawn. "Now, Pat, you got to be care-
ful out there," Nixon said, pumping my hand. "I was here for the
shah's funeral, and it was hot as hell." Also giving me a big smile
was Pat Haig. On Nixon's trips to Key Biscayne, I would snoop on
his staff at the Key Colony Hotel bar. There was a little band. If she
was there, I would dance with her. It would irritate Lieutenant Colonel Haig enough that he got press secretary Ron Ziegler to cut in.
"You're pumping her for information," Ziegler said.

Unlike Nixon and Pat, Haig greeted me with a deepening scowl.
In all the years, I cannot recall him with a smile. At our first meeting,
he was a military aide to Henry Kissinger, then adviser on national
security affairs. It was 1969, Nixon's first year in office. I wanted
Kissinger's briefing on Nixon's plans to end the war in Vietnam—a
central campaign pledge. Kissinger noted that Haig had served in
the war as a combat infantry officer. "Al, tell him our policy for
Vietnam," Kissinger said. Haig's eyes narrowed. "We're going to
win," he said. Kissinger grinned. Now the scowling Haig had ascended to be secretary of state, the number-one plum for any president to award. As president, Nixon had a warm relationship with
Reagan, making sure the California governor got assigned to foreign missions that would include his wife, Nancy. So President-elect

Reagan studied the memo from Nixon that said Haig was the only qualified one for the top job. "He is intelligent, strong, and generally shares your views on foreign policy," Nixon wrote five days after Reagan's election. "Those who oppose him are either ignorant or stupid." Reagan had been leaning toward George Shultz, a veteran Republican cabinet member who had been advising him on foreign affairs during the 1980 campaign.

In Cairo, Haig's intense briefing of Nixon was interrupted by my arrival. It may have included rumors that Israel was planning an invasion of Lebanon. But Haig stressed he had no firm—"no specific"—information until a day after the funeral, when he met with Begin. "Begin then told me that Israel had begun planning a move into Lebanon that would not draw Syria into the conflict," Haig wrote years later. Then he spelled out the basis for American support for such an invasion. "Unless there is a major internationally recognized provocation, the United States will not support such an action," Haig told Begin, and President Reagan would echo this in the coming weeks. What Haig did not say was that an Israeli invasion of Lebanon would result in the cutoff of US military aid. In effect, Haig was giving Begin a green light, and Begin felt free to charge ahead. Within eight months, Begin had his provocation and Reagan's support for a war on Syria and 17 months of bloody turmoil in the Levant. Before he was fired, Haig played an intimate role in supporting the right-wing Jerusalem government's ambition to cripple Syria and change the map of the Mideast. It included US backing of the most vicious players in the region, who drenched American promises with the blood of a massacre. And it would end badly for 220 US Marines, 18 sailors, and three soldiers sent to Beirut by Ronald Reagan.

Outside, soldiers struggled in the heat to place Sadat's casket on a caisson drawn by six black horses. Three were ridden by soldiers in green berets. The coffin was covered in the red, white, and black flag of Egypt. Thick black leather straps lashed the coffin to the caisson. Just behind, soldiers carried black velvet cushions bearing Sadat's medals, gold and jewels glinting in the sunlight. Horse-mounted drums began setting the slow pace for the cortege. Leading the way was a cavalry officer on a prancing Arabian stallion. A marching band played a mournful tune.

Forming up for the half-mile walk to the burial tomb were Nixon, Kissinger, former president Ford, and Prime Minister Begin. Farther down the line was former president Carter, who enabled Sadat's peace treaty between Egypt and Israel. In terms of foreign affairs, the achievement made him the most able of the presidents on parade. As president, however, Carter was widely ridiculed and despised even by members of the Democratic Party. The peanut farmer from Plains sought to apply Sunday school ethics to a city awash in personal vices of alcohol, hanky-panky, and political payoffs. "You can't get a drink here," said Speaker Thomas "Tip" O'Neill as he stormed out of one White House reception. Carter was forever cutting Army Engineer projects, a favorite of congressmen promising to bring home the bacon. He cut back support prices for fellow farmers. Carter was unafraid of almost every interest group in Washington. Doing the right thing produced a bipartisan army of Carter opponents. The hostility led Senator Edward M. Kennedy to challenge Carter's reelection and divide the ranks of the Democratic Party. Along with runaway inflation and the American embassy staff being held hostage in Tehran, Kennedy's losing campaign set Carter up for a landslide loss to Republican Ronald Reagan in 1980.

From the outset of his presidency, Carter made Sadat and a Mideast peace a priority. As a Washington outsider, Carter quickly violated the rule against getting personally involved in Mideast peace efforts. They were a quagmire, a graveyard for American presidential ambitions that seemed to reinforce hatreds between regional political players. Carter came to the issue awash in its history and religion, like the Baptist deacon he was. As governor of Georgia, he took the grand tour of Israel with his wife, Rosalynn, and staff at the expense of the Israeli government. Jimmy and Rosalynn were stunned when they finally arrived at the banks of the Jordan.

"All our lives we had read about this river, studied and sung about it, so we visualized a mighty current with almost magical qualities," Carter wrote later. Instead the waters where John baptized Jesus were more of a creek. Infuriating and disgusting its Arab neighbors, Israel had diverted the headwaters of the Jordan for Jewish farmers. It was 1973, months before Sadat's Operation Full Moon. Carter was shown IDF hardware and troops trained by an ex–US Marine who imposed all the hardships of Parris Island, South Carolina. From Golda Meir, the chain-smoking prime minister, and senior cabinet members, Carter got a political primer. "No one should fear the Arabs," Carter was told. "They have been badly beaten and will have to sue for peace. The Arab oil weapon is not a real threat. They need dollars more than the world needs us."

Sadat's calls for peace with Israel were largely dismissed in Jerusalem until Carter became president. The Arab leader's mission took on muscle when Carter summoned Sadat and Begin to hash things out at Camp David, the 125-acre presidential retreat in the Catoctin Mountains of Maryland. The outline of an agreement was announced to the world in September of 1978. In Jerusalem, the Knesset approved a version of the peace agreement. It was all for show. Begin insisted that final approval required a vote of his cabinet. "And I am only one vote there," he told a frustrated Carter. In

March, Carter flew to Jerusalem to make one final effort to salvage the agreement. Once again, Begin balked. On the night of March 12, Carter's aides told journalists that failure loomed. Air Force One, the president's 707 jetliner, was fueled with 10,000 gallons—enough to fly directly to Washington. To Begin, it appeared the American president was giving up and ready to blame the Israeli prime minister for the disaster. Begin buckled. At breakfast March 13, Begin agreed to every final item listed by Carter. Only later that day did Begin realize he was outfoxed by Carter's threat to fly home in defeat. When Air Force One took off a few hours later, it dumped 5,000 gallons of jet fuel in the Mediterranean. Carter flew to Cairo to give Sadat the good news.

In the cortege, French president François Mitterrand walked near Prince Charles, the future king, in a powder-blue military uniform. The drums beat slowly. Carter, Ford, and Nixon all pulled abreast of me in the march. As we arrived at the reviewing stand where Sadat was gunned down, I pointed out bullet holes to Nixon. He alerted Carter and Ford. We all gawked. The Israeli prime minister was walking just behind. Menachem Begin was the first Jewish leader to show that Israel depended on the US Congress, not the American president. He displayed an open contempt for Ronald Reagan earlier that year after the president criticized Israel's annexation of the Golan Heights. The mountain region was seized from Syria in the 1967 Arab-Israeli war. "Are we a vassal state of yours?" Begin demanded. "Are we a banana republic? Are we fourteen-year-olds who, if they misbehave, get their wrists slapped?" Then Begin brandished the anti-Semitic card against the American president, the Israeli government's response to any and all critics. "No one will frighten the large and free Jewish community of the United States," Begin said. "No one will succeed in deterring them with anti-Semitic propaganda. They will stand by our side. This is the land of their forefathers, and they have a right and duty to support it." Reagan later dismissed Begin's "harsh" tone as arguments among friends.

When the funeral ended, the prickly, stiff-necked former guerrilla fighter scurried on foot to his nearby hotel in Nasser City. It was Saturday, and riding on Shabbat was frowned on. His gratitude to Sadat was overflowing, and only increased when Israel invaded Lebanon eight months later. Sadat's peace treaty ensured the most powerful of all Arab armies would not interfere with the ambitions of Begin—and Reagan—in the Levant.

3

A Vain Fantasy

On the Rhine River, on the eastern shore, atop a steep rock, there once lived a nymph named Lorelei. She dressed in white and wore a wreath of stars in her hair. She was exquisite, but more striking than her physical beauty was the song she sang—a song so alluring, no one could resist its pull. People said that anyone sailing close to that rock would lose his life, for her song was irresistible, and no sailors who tried to reach Lorelei ever returned.

—German folktale

The Mideast version of this story involves three cadaverous Christian leaders—Gemayel, Chamoun, Franjieh—clinging to the mountain rocks of Lebanon. Facing certain death from surrounding Arab enemies, they sang to the Jews of Israel: Come form a coalition of Jews and Maronite Christians that will rule the Levant. David Ben-Gurion, the first prime minister of Israel, was lured by the song from Lebanon's minority sect. So was his one-eyed general, Moshe Dayan. "A Jewish-Christian front in the Arab ocean," Ben-Gurion proclaimed. They would buy a Christian leader who, in turn, would invite Israel to Beirut, and soon the Druse, the Shiites, and the Sunnis—the Islamic majority—would be under a Jewish-Christian thumb. And Lebanon's 6 million produced the most exotic fruits, wheat, barley, and the finest hashish in the region. Beirut was the Paris of the Mideast. What an acquisition! However, Israeli foreign minister Moshe Sharett delivered stinging face-slaps to Ben-Gurion and Dayan. "A vain fantasy," Sharett lectured. "We'll get bogged down in a mad adventure that will only bring us disgrace." In Arab Lebanon, no Christian dare embrace Israel or be a genuine ally, he said. Ben-Gurion backed off.

Sharett knew the Christian leaders for what they were: men without character or integrity scrambling to survive by sheer guile and the incompetence of Arab enemies. "Despicable" was how Egyptian president Anwar Sadat branded the Christian leadership. Cease-fires and peace agreements even within the Christian community were broken at the first opportunity to destroy neighboring families. Many massacres of Arab villages or communal bloodbaths somehow involved Christian knives.

Yet 25 years later the song of the Christians was heard once again. A Lebanon controlled by a Christian-Jewish axis seemed do-able to some of the most powerful men in the world. This time it lured President Ronald Reagan; his secretary of state, Alexander Haig; and his director of central intelligence, William Casey. They embraced a very unholy alliance designed by Menachem Begin, the prime minister of Israel, and his chief military adviser, Ariel Sharon. By 1982, the United States and Israel embarked together on a war to drive the Palestine Liberation Organization and Syria from Lebanon and to remake the map of the Levant. As Minister Sharett predicted, it was an adventure full of madness that brought defeat and a blood-drenched disgrace to the United States and Israel.

Since its founding in 1948, Israel had had a backdoor relationship with the Christians of Lebanon. The most extensive support for the Christians came in 1974 after Yitzhak Rabin succeeded Golda

Meir as Labor's prime minister. As fighting between the Palestine Liberation Organization and other factions developed in Lebanon, Rabin formulated a nonintervention policy. He began supplying large amounts of military hardware to the Christians—US M-16 rifles, antitank missiles, old but working Sherman tanks. "Our guiding principle," Rabin told one Christian leader, "is that we are prepared to help you help yourselves."

Begin and Sharon changed that policy. This time, the prime minister and *mon general* had picked out a Christian warlord to change the map of the Mideast. He was Bashir Gemayel, 31, the youngest son of warlord Pierre Gemayel. Pierre, an admirer of Francisco Franco in Spain and other fascists, organized a militia in East Beirut and named it the Phalange. Bashir was educated by Jesuits in Beirut—members of the order had been dispatched by Rome two centuries earlier when there was a tenuous tie to Pope Clement XII—but he and most other Lebanese Christians were adherents of the Eastern-rite Maronite church. Bashir spent time in the United States attending a college in Texas and working for a law firm in Washington, DC. In the Phalange militia, he could be both erratic and impulsive—two traits that worried his father. Even so, Pierre made Bashir commander of the family militia in 1976 as civil war engulfed them.

Two years later, the longtime rivalry between the Gemayels and Suleiman Franjieh spun out of control. Franjieh, a Christian leader and former president of Lebanon, refused to join Bashir's military forces in the Lebanon civil war. As a result, 200 of Bashir's troops attacked the Franjieh summer home. Sulieman's son Tony and Tony's wife and three-year-old daughter were killed, along with 28 other persons. Both Pierre Gemayel and his older brother, Amin, were reportedly outraged by Bashir's massacre. Bashir, boyish, short, and stocky, with a great smile and personal magnetism, was beyond family control. His goal was to unite all warring Christian militias under his command, no matter the cost. Bashir himself was the target of assassination in February of 1980. Instead, a bomb planted in his Mercedes killed his 20-month-old daughter, Maya. Five months later, Bashir settled his final score. This time it was the Tiger Army of Camille Chamoun, like Franjieh a former Christian president of Lebanon. (A 1943 French mandate dictated a "confessional arrangement" of political leadership, always allotting the presidency to a Christian.) Bashir directed his Phalange forces against all Chamoun operations, including storefronts, in East Beirut. A second assault was on a beach resort where the Chamoun family had a home. Bashir's machine gunners turned a seaside marina swimming pool red with the blood of bathers. Doctors later reported many bodies were mutilated: Sex organs and tongues were cut out. Owners of the seaside marina were tortured before being killed—one blown up with dynamite, the other hacked in half. At least 300 people died that day.

Bashir Gemayel's trail of blood did not bother Begin and Sharon, who had differing perceptions of the young warlord. To Begin, Bashir represented a repressed minority in Lebanon threatened with extinction. Time and again, Begin said he supported Christians in Lebanon to prevent "genocide." To him, it seemed the Christians were kin to the Jews in the Warsaw ghetto facing the Nazis. In their meetings, Bashir would seemingly acquiesce to everything Begin, at 67 years old, requested. "How could I possibly refuse such a venerable old man," Bashir said. But after the session, when Begin's aides sought to confirm details, Bashir insisted he was misquoted and would later deny the whole agreement. The young warlord was duplicitous in almost every deal with the Israelis. Yet Begin continued to dote on the smiling, obsequious Bashir. When the Israeli government demanded the wealthy Christians in Lebanon begin paying for Jerusalem's weapon supplies, Bashir quickly agreed. However, he sought—and received—a 50 percent discount from the Israeli army for a $2 million purchase. Then Bashir complained that he was being nagged for another $1 million. Begin waived away the additional payment by the beaming Bashir. Israel sucked up the expense.

"Bashir, when he wasn't murdering people, was a likable man," said Robert Dillon, US ambassador to Beirut. "He had great boyish charm."

Sharon viewed Bashir in military terms. Rather than being put off by attacks on Christian rivals, Sharon approved Bashir's drive to unify Christian forces in Lebanon. To Sharon, the collective Christian militia would be crucial to his invasion of Lebanon. Once Israeli forces routed the Syrian army—Damascus was certain to intervene—Sharon planned to seize control of the Beirut-Damascus highway. That would break Syrian president Hafez al-Assad's control of Beirut. And that would leave Israeli troops surrounding Palestine Liberation Organization fighters in southern Lebanon. Sharon would be on the edge of West Beirut, the headquarters for the PLO and its leader, Yasser Arafat. From its base in East Beirut, Bashir's forces—backed by Israel—would clean the PLO from West Beirut. "Leave West Beirut to us," Bashir told Sharon. With the PLO expelled and Syria defeated, a new Lebanon would be born.

For both Begin and Sharon, the endgame of a 1982 Lebanon invasion would mean claiming the lost gold of El Dorado. It was an election year in Lebanon, and with the support of Israeli invaders, Bashir Gemayel would be voted into the presidency by the Lebanese parliament. Then he would make a dramatic visit to Jerusalem—in Anwar Sadat's footsteps—which would be followed by a peace treaty. Israel would for the first time have a primary role in an Arab country.

Most experts on the Mideast perceived the Israeli plan to be not only too ambitious and risky but also downright delusional, more cockamamie than credible. Syrian president Assad had had 35,000 troops in Lebanon since 1976. He planned to annex the country to Syria. With his Soviet-supplied military, Assad would fight any Israeli presence to the last man in Lebanon. Within senior ranks of the Israel Defense Forces, Bashir Gemayel was perceived as the weakest link in the plan. Bashir was an untrustworthy fraud who would abandon his Jerusalem mentors at the most important moments. He commanded not combat-ready soldiers so much as layabout thugs quick to drive knives into the softest targets. Sharon's invasion of Lebanon would destroy Israel's global image. No longer would Israel be seen as a small country surrounded by powerful Arabs. Instead, an attack on Lebanon and Beirut would project a Jewish military superpower that threatened all. The weapons that would be used against Syria and Lebanon were American supplied. Would President Ronald Reagan tolerate such an aggressive Israel? The short answer was yes. In 1983, Reagan was on an anti-Communist tear funding what he called "freedom fighters" opposed to Russian-backed governments in Afghanistan, Angola, Nicaragua—wherever Communist influence could be rolled back. That included the PLO and Syria, both armed and supplied by the Kremlin. And that red menace in the Mideast was what Haig pitched to the Kremlin-baiting president of the United States.

Israel's shift from defender to invader did not seem to bother Alexander Haig. Sharon laid it all out in a two-hour meeting with the secretary of state in May of 1982—a month before the invasion. Haig arranged for senior department officials to attend Sharon's briefing and measure the bulky, noisy, white-haired general of the Jewish legions. Haig, himself a retired four-star general, admired Sharon's swagger. Sharon at first focused on ending the PLO threat in southern Lebanon. For the first time, they heard of a 40-kilometer incursion that would wrap up in two days. That was the bogus cover story Haig and Begin outlined to the public shortly after the invasion began.

"Our intention is not a large operation," Sharon said at first. "We will try to be as small and efficient as possible."

"Like a lobotomy," Haig interjected.

Then the Foggy Bottom briefing revealed Sharon's bigger ambitions. Sharon's code name for it was Operation Big Pines, an allusion to the giant cedar in the middle of the flag of Lebanon. "We do not intend to attack Syria, but it is almost impossible to act without hitting the Syrians," Sharon said. "Our aim is not to see to the constitution of a free Lebanon or to drive the Syrians out, but these may be by-products of the action."

"How far will you go?" asked one US official.

"As far as we have to," Sharon replied.

While cautioning Sharon, Haig repeatedly agreed when the defense minister insisted Israel alone could decide on military actions to protect its national security. To some at the meeting, Haig was telling Sharon he could do whatever he felt necessary.

Also attending was Philip Habib, the president's Mideast representative. Habib was already struggling with the Jerusalem government and the PLO. Haig's tone with Sharon worried him. Habib noisily opposed Sharon's more expansive plans for Lebanon.

"The thing about the Israelis is if you don't make your opposition unalterably clear, they will take it as acquiescence," Habib's deputy, Morris Draper, said. "If you don't tell them no, they take it for yes." Habib saw Haig giving Sharon the green light to invade Lebanon. After the meeting, Habib approached Haig and told him Sharon thought he had received "an OK from us to run an operation into Lebanon."

That spring, not everyone in Washington was ready to rubberstamp the Israeli plan. Sharon had asked Director of Central Intelligence Casey for $10 million for Bashir Gemayel. While Casey favored the secret payment, his deputy, Navy Admiral Bobby Inman, balked. Inman held the informed view from the CIA station in Beirut—Bashir cared only for Bashir. Frustrated by Inman's opposition, Casey appealed to Reagan. Sharon appealed to Haig, and Haig convinced Reagan. The president signed a secret "finding" approving the $10 million. The finding is still classified in the archives of Reagan's Presidential Library.

By September, everyone in Washington would regret the funding of the Phalange forces and the legacy of Bashir Gemayel.

4

Mole Cricket

North of the Sea of Galilee, I took a break from war reporting. It was June 9—the third day of the 1982 Israeli invasion of Lebanon—and I had just left an Israel Defense Forces battalion moving slowly north on foot. I pulled over to inhale the perfume of northern Israel. The fragrance from eucalyptus trees filled the cooler air. The sunlight, free of city dust, made brilliant every flower and leaf. And the sky . . .

Wait a minute.

Above, the blue sky to my west was full of supersonic aircraft in a classic air battle. Just to the south, an E-2C Hawkeye was loitering on a racetrack course. This US Navy version of airborne warning and control (AWAC) was orchestrating an air battle for the Israeli air force. Two F-15C Eagles were roaring north with fiery afterburners. Coming south was an F-16 Falcon spiraling in a joyful victory barrel roll. The black puff of an exploding missile warhead was seen but not heard. For me, it was a silent airshow of America's most powerful aerial weapons in the hands of the Israeli air force in a full-bore attack on Russian jets flown by Syrian pilots. As a Pentagon reporter in Washington, I instantly grasped the rarity of 200 warplanes filling the blue sky. Not since the Korean War of 1950 had Russian and American jets engaged in battle, and then nothing on the scale unfolding above. But the politics of the battle baffled.

The details of that day during the summer of 1982 would not become clear for several years. Misleading statements and downright lies by both the American and Israeli governments put a cloak of duplicity over what became known as the Bekaa Valley Turkey Shoot. The day before, June 8, 1982, Prime Minister Menachem Begin took the floor of the Israeli parliament, the Knesset, for a rare direct appeal to Syrian president Hafez al-Assad.

"I once again state that we do not want a war with Syria," Begin said. "From this platform I call on President Assad to instruct the Syrian army not to harm Israeli soldiers, and then nothing bad will happen to [Syrian soldiers]. We desire no clashes with the Syrian army. If we reach the line 40 kilometers from our northern border the work will have been done, all fighting will end. I am directing my words to the ears of the president of Syria."

It was a total ruse. Begin never announced Israel's war on Syria as the Jerusalem government did on the Palestine Liberation Organization on May 4.

Israel's ambassador to London, Shlomo Argov, was attacked and shot—he recovered months later—on May 3, 1982. The attack was ordered by Abu Nidal, leader of Fatah and the archenemy of Yasser Arafat, head of the Palestine Liberation Organization. Nidal had left the PLO after bitter attacks on Arafat. Members of the Begin cabinet had second thoughts about blaming Arafat for the London attack when Abu Nidal's role was clear. But Begin shut off debate. "They're all PLO," the prime minister said. Begin approved air strikes on 255 of Arafat's PLO sites in southern Lebanon and Beirut. Hundreds were killed and injured. Arafat replied the next day with a 24-hour barrage of rockets on northern Israel. The war was under way.

The very next day after Begin's Knesset appeal to the Syrian president, Begin and his defense minister, Ariel Sharon, implemented Operation Mole Cricket. The strike, two years in the planning, was designed to strip Syria of its air force and drive 35,000 Syrian troops out of Lebanon. Without air support, the Syrian forces that had occupied Lebanon for seven years would be easy pickings for Israeli armored and air forces. Syria's defeat and the expulsion of PLO fighters would permit Jerusalem to redraw the Mideast map. That fall, Begin planned to install as president of Lebanon the Christian warlord Bashir Gemayel. In turn, Gemayel would sign a peace treaty and open diplomatic and trade relations with the Jewish nation. It was exactly the game plan Begin outlined to Secretary of State Alexander Haig three years earlier in Cairo. Haig enlisted the support of President Ronald Reagan.

In the sky over Lebanon's Bekaa Valley on June 9, America's most important weapons were put on display by an Israeli government that defied American restrictions on their use. While the combat planes, electronic warfare aircraft, and all-seeing radar had been given for Israel's defense, now Begin and Sharon were using the weapons for all-out aggression—a first for Israel. At every turn, American weapons crippled and then crushed Syria's air defenses and air force. Mole Cricket began at 2 p.m. June 9, with Israeli and American drones teasing crucial electronic signatures from the warheads of Soviet-made surface-to-air missiles. These were the very same Soviet SAMs that wrecked the Israeli air force nine years earlier in the Yom Kippur War. This time, Syrian SAM batteries mistook the drones for attacking aircraft. When they "painted" the drones, their radar signatures were relayed to following American F-4 Phantoms that popped up over the SAM batteries. US antiradiation missiles were quickly armed with the SAM signatures from the drones. These US missiles zoomed down an electronic highway to destroy the first of 26 Syrian batteries. These were American tactics refined in Vietnam to combat massive Soviet SAM networks all over Hanoi.

The Hawkeye AWAC system—its radar covered 3 million cubic miles—spotted Syrian air force turmoil. Syrians flying Soviet MiG-20s and MiG-21s took off from Shayrat Airbase, and Hawkeye instantly assigned F-15s and F-16s on an interception course. These vectoring US warplanes were armed with American Sidewinder air-to-air rockets. No need to maneuver behind the enemy. Launched from any angle miles away, the supersonic Sidewinders destroyed Syrian pilots who were unaware of an attack until too late. Over two days, Israeli pilots shot down 86 Syrian MiGs, some at a range of 10 miles. Only one F-15 was damaged. And 26 SAM batteries were destroyed without a single F-4 Phantom loss. In Damascus, Syrian generals were unable to get a clear picture of the attack. A major reason was a US-made electronic-warfare Boeing 707 hovering over the battlefield, filled with gear that jammed radar and both radio and telephone transmission in Syria. More than 100 Syrian MiGs entered the fray over two days but without radar guidance. Benjamin Lambeth of the RAND Corporation saw the unguided Syrian MiG-21s. "I watched a group of Syrian fighter planes fly figure-eights," he said. "They just flew around and around and obviously had no idea what to do next."

Just as isolated from the air war 30 miles away was Phillip Habib, President Reagan's personal Mideast representative. He was waiting at the American embassy in Damascus for a meeting with Syrian president Assad. Habib was carrying a cease-fire plan from Israel, his stock-in-trade. Throughout the 10-year war in Vietnam and later in other countries, Habib had become the star US negotiator, arbitrator, interlocutor, and brilliant policymaker. Habib's reputation was a major reason he was recruited by Haig and Reagan. The son of Lebanese immigrants, Habib was a tough-talking product of Brooklyn who used unvarnished directness with everyone. That delighted Ronald Reagan, who used ethnic jokes that had Habib laughing through many of their meetings in 1982. Quickly, Habib realized Reagan had more misinformation than knowledge about the Mideast. The president was convinced that the turmoil in Lebanon was caused by the Soviet Union and that Moscow was using Syria and the PLO to threaten Israel. The air defense missiles in Lebanon were really Syria's warheads aiming at Israel. White House staffers prepared 3"×5" cards with Mideast details that Reagan would read aloud during policy sessions. The president retained nothing. According to Habib, his boss "couldn't remember one detail from one minute to the next." But for the Big Picture, Reagan shared with Haig the determination that America would protect Israel—no matter what.

Habib was no Mideast whiz. He had carried to Damascus a cease-fire proposal from Begin that Syrian experts at the State Department and Central Intelligence Agency knew Assad would never accept. It required Syria to pull its troops out of southern Lebanon, along with its air defense missiles. Habib met with Assad amid the roar of Syrian jets from a nearby airbase. Assad offered no hint that he knew Israeli warplanes had launched the Mole Cricket attack at 2 p.m. When Habib returned to the Damascus embassy, he learned of Begin's massive air attack. Habib quickly arranged for a second

meeting with Assad. He found the Syrian president tense and suspi-
cious of the representative of the American president. No matter
what was said, Habib realized the skills that won plaudits in Asia
were useless in the Mideast. Habib that night cabled Washington:
"I am astounded and dismayed by what happened today. The prime
minister of Israel in reality sent me off on a wild goose chase."

Mole Cricket's total destruction was certainly a military disaster for Syria. It was also a deep wound for Assad, a Soviet-trained
jet fighter pilot and commander of the air force before becoming
president. Assad began preaparing for a Mideast-style revenge that
would stun both Israel and the United States. It would take time.
He would later portray Habib as an agent of Israel, not the United
States. After accusing Habib of deception about a later cease-fire
with Israel, Assad declared Habib persona non grata, the ultimate
slap in a diplomat's face, ending his welcome in Damascus.

Habib's initial foray in the Mideast had been a disaster. There
were more to come.

5

The Siege

Arriving aboard the night ferry from Cyprus, it seemed a fire-works display was under way over Lebanon's capital, Beirut. Getting closer to Beirut harbor, however, the ferry was more a combat landing ship heading for Omaha Beach. White phosphorous warheads exploded with a halo of white stars over West Beirut. One of these white flecks of what the military called Willie Pete would burn flesh to the bone. Fiery aerial bombs destroyed whole apartment buildings. Naval guns offshore kept up a constant barrage that rattled the deck of the arriving Cyprus ferry. Near the Corniche of West Beirut, home to the US embassy, artillery and tanks pounded with a roar that shook the Muslim sector. It was once the seaside promenade for Beirut lovers and families. Once the Paris of the Mideast, Beirut was now shell-shocked. The 56-day Israeli siege of West Beirut was at its thundering peak that August night. Ariel Sharon, minister of defense of the Jerusalem government, was in battle dress in East Beirut and directing the bombardment. The man Prime Minister Menachem Begin called *mon general* had become unhinged. Begin and the Israeli cabinet could no longer control—if they ever did—the rotund Sharon. His elaborate ambition to conquer Lebanon had degenerated into a single-minded and merciless pounding of Muslim Beirut. As his frustrations mounted, his appetite added more to his 300-pound body. "He cleaned out everything in the kitchen," said one East Beirut restaurateur. A month earlier, the white-haired Sharon had cut off electricity and water in West Beirut and scoured the streets for PLO leader Yasser Arafat. Israeli agents—mainly Christian soldiers from Bashir Gemayel's Phalange militia—staged terrorist attacks. Car bombs were installed and detonated throughout West Beirut streets. Transponders that could send signals to Israeli receivers were planted in buildings suspected to house Arafat and other PLO leaders. Loitering Israeli warplanes would then attack these electronically pinpointed targets. Arafat always managed to escape. In one case, on August 6, rumors quickly spread that he had left only minutes before an American-made laser-guided bomb destroyed two eight-floor apartment buildings and the more than 200 people in it. One of the buildings had once housed the PLO's security headquarters. Only a week after the June 6 invasion, it seemed the PLO was finished. The PLO strongholds and refugee camps near Tyre, Sidon, and other southern Lebanon towns were surrounded and bombarded. The PLO strongpoint in Beaufort Castle, the twelfth-century Crusader castle that overlooked all southern Lebanon, was overrun. A surrounded Arafat, refused military aid by both Syria and Moscow, hinted he might accept exile from Lebanon. All that changed. Many senior PLO commanders deserted fighters in southern Lebanon to hide in West Beirut. Soon, PLO fighters shed uniforms and melted into the population of West Beirut. As the siege grew in intensity, Arafat became more defiant of demands made by Sharon and US diplomats. Arafat and his soldiers went underground in West Beirut, where bunkers could withstand aerial bombardment. Two American reporters scrambling for safety in one bombardment jumped into an unlit underground bunker. They were welcomed by the sound of bullets being racked into dozens of Kalashnikov rifles. They were spared after shouting, *"Sahafi! Sahafi!"*—the Arab word for "press." During the day, West Beirut was drowned by the sounds of electric generators wired to every storefront. While I was away, a wayward howitzer damaged my regular room at the Commodore Hotel in West Beirut. Still, after arriving on the Cyprus ferry, I spent the night in the room. After all, what were the chances of another direct hit? I awoke the next morning to repairmen on ladders patching the 105 mm hole. Reporters from the entire world were hunkered down at the Commodore. Coco, the hotel's poolside parrot, added a new sound to its vocabulary of curses. It was a high-to-low whistle that perfectly mimicked an incoming warhead.

Coverage of the bombardment in the print media and on television led to relentless condemnation of Israel from all corners of the world. Holocaust survivors in Germany pleaded with Israel to halt the inhumanity. NBC News anchor John Chancellor likened the siege to the Fascist bombing of Madrid during the Spanish Civil War. Instead of America's vital ally in the Mideast, Chancellor saw a regional aggressor armed by the United States. "We are now dealing with an imperial Israel," he said. "Israel can't go on much longer horrifying the world." Israeli spokesmen argued that the press was distorting the siege. Television showed some of the thousands killed and injured, including a baby at a Beirut hospital with its arms blown off. Sharon's siege destroyed support for the antiterrorist drive called Operation Peace for Galilee. Instead of reinforcing Israel's portrayal of the Palestine Liberation Organization as ruthless terrorists, the siege revived sympathy for Palestinians. Arafat and others were driven from their Palestine homeland with the creation of Israel in 1948. After the 1967 war, Israel seized the West Bank of the Jordan and chased the PLO to the East Bank, where they attempted to overthrow the Jordanian government. Once more, Arafat and the PLO were defeated and expelled from Jordan with their families. More than 200,000 Palestinians traveled through Syria to southern Lebanon. At every stage of the diaspora, Arafat staged attacks on Israel. And Israel always struck back.

Operation Big Pines, Sharon's 1982 plan to expel Syria from Lebanon and destroy the Palestine Liberation Organization once and for all, had collapsed on three fronts. A determined Assad and the narrow dirt roads of Lebanon's Bekaa Valley blocked Sharon's plan to sever the main highway between Beirut and Damascus midway between the two capitals. That would outflank 35,000 Syrian troops who had occupied Lebanon since 1976. Instead, narrow mountain roads hamstrung the main battle tank columns of the Israel Defense Forces. Refueling trucks couldn't get through. Some armor units ran out of gasoline. Scores of IDF tanks sent to attack Assad's army were unable to maneuver on the narrow roads and never fired their guns. IDF units hemmed in on narrow valley roads came under Syrian fire above them on ridgelines. Abandoned villages came alive with Syrian troops when Israeli tanks came within range. Soviet-made Sagger handheld rockets picked off IDF tanks in one valley clash. For the first time, IDF armor came under fire from French-made helicopters with Syrian pilots firing laser-guided antitank rockets from four miles away—well beyond IDF antiaircraft defenses.

Syria's counterattack forced Sharon to forsake the Bekaa Valley and shift strategy to surrounding Beirut and trapping the PLO leadership and Syrian occupying troops. The June 14 maneuver was never approved, before or after, by the Israeli cabinet. Also balking were some Israeli commanders in the IDF citizen army. Sharon's order was defied by Colonel Eli Geva, a tank brigade commander, one of the best and brightest of the IDF's younger officers. He refused an order from the chief of staff to take his tanks into West Beirut and resigned from the army. He said entry would bog the tanks down in urban warfare and endanger civilians.

Israeli soldiers, like the world, were told the invasion would halt 40 kilometers into southern Lebanon and focus attack on PLO sites along the west coast. Now Sharon was violating a tenet of Israeli foreign policy: Never occupy an Arab capital. Sharon's base of operation was in East Beirut, where the IDF linked with the Phalange, the Christian militia under the command of Bashir Gemayel. The ruthless young warlord was crucial to Sharon's endgame: In the coming fall election, Israel would back Gemayel as the next president of Lebanon in the face of little opposition. In turn, Gemayel would sign a peace treaty with Israel, giving the Jerusalem government a dominating role in Lebanese affairs. The possible redrawing of the map of Lebanon was secretly supported by Secretary of State Alexander Haig, who had enlisted President Reagan in financing the Phalange with $10 million. Sharon called on Gemayel in East Beirut to collect on the warlord's promise: Once Beirut was surrounded, Gemayel said, his militia would wade into West Beirut and slaughter the PLO in house-to-house fighting. Begin had promised Israeli military support for the bloodletting but insisted the Phalange lead the way. "Let me take care of West Beirut" was Gemayel's assurance during the planning stage. Now Gemayel refused. If—as planned—he was elected president of a Muslim-majority country, Gemayel said, he would be unable to govern with West Beirut's blood on his hands. Without the Phalange, Sharon had only the siege. While the Israeli generals had drawn up a plan for the bloody invasion of West Beirut, Begin would have no part of it. The prime minister genuinely grieved for every Israeli killed on the battlefield.

In addition to Syria's counterattack and Bashir Gemayel's refusal to invade West Beirut, Sharon found that the televised siege was eroding crucial support of some in Washington. There was no wavering by Alexander Haig. The secretary of state had remained staunch. Haig even read to Washington newsmen Israeli government statements minimizing death and destruction in West Beirut. Robert Dillon, the American ambassador to Lebanon, witnessed daily destruction from his hillside residence in East Beirut. Dillon called the State Department to denounce the ferocity of Israel's jets and artillery in an area full of innocent civilians. Haig, an Army veteran of the US air war in Vietnam, dismissed Dillon's alarms. "Bullshit," Haig said. "There wasn't any heavy Israeli bombing. It was fringe bombing. In the siege of Beirut, there was not a massive bombing at all." Compared to America's bombing of Hanoi in 1972, Sharon's bombardments were "more token than real."

Sharon and Haig found themselves increasingly outflanked by Philip Habib, President Reagan's personal Mideast representative. New to the Mideast, the career diplomat found himself manipulated by Prime Minister Begin and bullied by Sharon. "Sharon is a brawny man who uses his bulk, his extremely loud voice and a flagrantly aggressive manner which I suspect he has cultivated for effect to overwhelm opposition," Haig recalled. Sharon would actually bump into a person in his face-to-face confrontations. In conversation, Sharon called Habib naïve and America weak. Habib

thought Sharon a bully and a liar. An undiplomatic loathing for
Sharon arose in Habib. "Philip hated Arik Sharon with a deep, dark
passion," said Marjorie, Habib's wife (Arik was a nickname for Sharon's first name, Ariel).

Although he was the new boy on the block in the Mideast, the
62-year-old diplomat was a wily veteran of Washington politics.
Reagan had endorsed Habib's central focus of nailing down a cease-
fire to halt Israel's attacks. His initiatives were blocked by Haig.
Samuel Lewis, US ambassador to Israel at the time, watched the
increasingly hostile relationship between Habib and his boss at the
State Department. "Habib didn't like Haig very much. Didn't respect him. Why? Disagreed with him. Thought he was a kind of
megalomaniac and very pro-Israeli and not a very good diplomat."
To get around Haig, the president's special representative to the
Mideast appealed to his second boss, President Reagan, or, more
specifically, Reagan's daily advisers—Edwin Meese, William Clark,
James Baker, and Mike Deaver. Habib's briefings for them were detailed and weekly. Their dislike of Haig began on the day of Reagan's inauguration. Haig showed up with a letter to be signed by the
president. It restricted all foreign policy decisions to Haig, cutting
out the White House National Security Council. It was the same
sort of power Henry Kissinger possessed while secretary of state and
adviser on national security affairs to President Nixon. While he
learned much as Kissinger's deputy, Haig never gained the same
stature with Reagan. The letter went unsigned. Haig proclaimed
himself as Reagan's foreign policy "vicar." As a fervent Catholic,
he was likening his role to the pope of Rome, who represents God
on earth. From then on, every State Department reporter referred
to Haig as "The Vicar." With every real or imagined infringement on

his turf by the White House, Haig would complain bitterly to Reagan, often with the added threat of resignation. The president, who loathed infighting among his staff, always placated Haig.

With news reporters and associates, Haig never hid his contempt for Reagan's closest advisers or the president himself. He had constant criticism for Reagan's national security adviser, William Clark. At every turn in his political career Reagan brought along Clark, a California rancher with a law degree. Clark was in fact the president's best friend, free to wander into the Oval Office no matter the topic or already-present visitor. At one point Reagan made him a justice of the California Supreme Court. In Washington, Haig made Clark deputy secretary of state because of his connection with Reagan. When the national security post became open, Clark quickly returned to the White House. He designed the Mini-Memo. No matter the issue, it was reduced to a single page for Reagan's desk. Reagan preferred the visual and loved film. The Pentagon film library was searched for training films suitable to educate the president about, say, the Soviet Union. Clark himself shared Reagan's disinterest in world affairs. Clark "didn't know his ass from third base," Haig grumbled. "How could he? He never read a book on foreign policy in his life." He saw Reagan in the same boat, at sea and unengaged with the facts of a serious problem. "He wasn't a mean man. He was just stupid," Clark quoted Haig saying of Reagan. Other senior officials held the same view, including William Casey, director of central intelligence. While Reagan was indeed smart enough to become president of the United States, he remained uninterested in foreign facts that Haig, Casey, and others considered vital. Reagan hated war and violence and urged Habib to do everything to bring peace to the Mideast.

Reagan's attitude toward Israel's invasion of Lebanon began to change after Vice President George H. W. Bush and Defense Secretary Caspar Weinberger attended the June funeral of Saudi Arabia's King Kalid in Riyadh. The Saudis were convinced the United States supported the Israeli invasion of Lebanon, the destruction of Syria's air force, and, just then, the start of Sharon's siege of West Beirut. The ruthless attack on the Muslim quarter had every Islamic center seething. The undertone of the Saudis' objections hinted at another embargo of oil shipments to the United States. Bush and Weinberger brought word of the possible catastrophe back to the White House. Ten years earlier, the Saudis had destroyed the American economy with an oil embargo and runaway inflation. Suddenly, Saudi sensitivities were injected into deliberations about Lebanon. Saudi prince Bandar bin Sultan gained the ear of Clark, Reagan's national security adviser, and began pushing the US cease-fire plan with Syrian president Assad. He became an important channel between the White House and the PLO's Yasser Arafat. When Haig got wind of Clark possibly undercutting State Department control of policy toward Arafat, he took his outrage to the Oval Office. Reagan listened. "Utterly paranoid" was his later judgment.

After the first full week of Sharon's siege, Begin showed up in the Oval Office on June 21. The day before, Begin sought a temporary halt in the bombing of West Beirut. On the phone, Sharon refused, invoking his blanket excuse for all his actions: I have to protect our men. Haig had prepared the prime minister for the meeting with the American president. "Hold out for what you want," Haig advised Begin. Begin opened by spotlighting Israel's destruction of the Syrian air force on June 9. "The combination of American planes and Israeli pilots is an excellent commercial symbol," Begin said. It was an allusion to multimillion-dollar US sales of warplanes to other nations. Reagan jumped to the ravaging of West Beirut. The president acknowledged the seriousness of the attack on Israel's ambassador to London. "I was pretty blunt," Reagan wrote in his diary. He doubted the attack "warranted the retaliation which has taken so many lives in Lebanon." He urged Begin to move forward on the diplomatic front. "What's done is done," Reagan said. Reagan wanted Israel to join Syria in withdrawing forces from Lebanon, but he did not insist. The president was still supporting Israel's strategy of ousting Syria and installing Bashir Gemayel as president of Lebanon. Even his fiery representative in the Mideast, Habib, favored the Gemayel endgame.

"It's a complex problem," Reagan wrote. "While we think his action was overkill it still may turn out to be the best opportunity we've had to reconcile the warring factions in Lebanon." The wishful thinking reflected what the US intelligence community saw as a profound ignorance of Lebanon in the highest circles of the Reagan administration. Begin had gotten what he wanted from Reagan. The siege of Beirut raged on for six more weeks.

Haig, the architect of American support for Begin and Sharon since 1981, was toppled by one final temper tantrum. Three days after the Begin meeting, Haig submitted to the president a list of wrongs against the secretary of state by the White House staff. Their meeting also included orders from Haig to Habib that had not been approved by Reagan. In confronting Haig, Reagan asked what General Haig would do if a lower commander ignored his orders. "I would fire him," Haig replied. The next day in the Oval Office, Reagan handed him an unsealed envelope. Inside was an unsigned letter of resignation for Haig. Haig asked for time to write his own letter noting their disagreements over major foreign policy issues. Reagan simply announced Haig's resignation at the afternoon press briefing. "Actually, the only disagreement was over whether I made policy or the Sec. of State did," Reagan wrote later. Haig was not quite finished. While George Shultz was named to replace him, Reagan had asked Haig to stay on until Shultz was confirmed by the Senate. In a huff, Haig decamped with his family to the Greenbrier, a luxury hotel in the mountains of West Virginia. All the secretary's business—including orders to Habib—was relayed by phone and telex from the hotel 240 miles from Washington. The Vicar was finally defrocked on July 9, when a phone call from Reagan interrupted Haig in the ornate Greenbrier dining room. The president agreed with Shultz that Haig should turn over authority to an acting secretary. "Very little more was said," Haig recounted. "I went in and finished my dinner."

In August, the siege worsened in West Beirut. The oil kingdom's renewed influence came in a telephone call to the White House two days after Sharon became unglued and ordered a 24-hour saturation bombing. At least 300 were killed. On August 12, the newly elevated King Fahd called from Riyadh. Reagan recounted the call in his diary. Fahd "was begging me to do something," Reagan wrote. "I told him I was calling P.M. Begin immediately. And I did—I was angry—I told him it had to stop or our entire future relationship was endangered. I used the word holocaust deliberately & said the symbol of the war was becoming a picture of a 7-month-old baby with its arms blown off."

Begin was stung. He had lost family in the Nazi purge of Jews in Poland. "The president said, 'It's a holocaust,'" Begin said. "He hurt me very deeply." Watching the telephone exchange in the prime minister's office was John Kifner of The New York Times. The furious Begin yelled to an aide to get "the picture." Begin showed the photo to Kifner. "That's a holocaust," Begin said. It showed a small boy in a newsboy hat with his hands up, walking under the guns of Polish and Nazi troops. Reagan's phone call stung enough that Begin cracked down on Sharon. He called a meeting of the cabinet. They voted to strip Sharon of authority to order air, sea, or ground attacks on West Beirut—without specific approval of Begin and the cabinet. It was the first of several Israeli government censures.

The king of Saudi Arabia was not the only Arab enraged by the combination of Sharon's ruthlessness and American weapons. Engineering classes were interrupted at the American University of Beirut for a 19-year-old Shiite Muslim. His name was Imad Mughniyeh, and the siege filled him with anger that would soon be translated into the destruction of the US embassy in Beirut and the bombing of a makeshift barracks where 241 Americans died. Watching the weeks of bombardment on television also fed the hatred of a wealthy Saudi, Osama bin Laden.

At the time, in 1982, bin Laden told the British journalist Robert Fiske in 2004, "After the situation became unbearable—and we witnessed the injustice and tyranny of the American-Israeli alliance against our people in Palestine and Lebanon—I thought about it. And the events that affected me directly were those of 1982 and the events that followed—when America allowed the Israelis to invade Lebanon, helped by the US Sixth Fleet. As I watched the destroyed towers in Lebanon, it occurred to me to punish the unjust the same way: to destroy towers in America so it could taste some of what we were tasting and to stop killing our children and women."

With growing support from the White House, Habib stepped up demands from Israel for a cease-fire. Since the Fourth of July, Habib had been formulating plans to expel the Arafat and PLO fighters from Beirut. To prevent Sharon from attacking the departing PLO, Habib was proposing a multinational military force to act as both protectors and escorts. Habib balked at including American forces in such a peacekeeping force. He was challenged by his deputy, Morris Draper. American forces were a must, Draper insisted.

Habib agreed. He proposed US Marines for the duty. Reagan quickly granted his approval.

6

Turmoil

The best laid schemes o' Mice an' Men
Gang aft agley
—ROBERT BURNS

Feathers from the giant black grouse of the Italian Alps stole the show. Long, shiny, and black, a spray was attached to the white combat helmets of the 2nd Battalion of the Bersaglieri. Then some of the 518 Italian sharpshooters arrived not in march step, not at the double, but at a flawless, syncopated dead run. Like their black plumes, the high-speed march had been their hallmark since their formation by the king of Sardinia in 1836. Their commander, Lieutenant Colonel Bruno Tosetti, was so handsome, and his troops so dramatic, the world's cameras collectively zoomed in on the beaming Bersaglieri. The Italians were the most colorful members of the multinational force created by the United States to protect the defeated Palestine Liberation Organization. French Foreign Legionnaires and American Marines wore only battlefield dress. They were mostly grim and meant business. The Italians' arrival took the edge off the daily pandemonium surrounding the expulsion of Yasser Arafat and 14,000 Palestinian Liberation Organization soldiers from Beirut in August of 1982. The French, Italian, and American troops, an instant Multinational Defense Force assembled hurriedly by US negotiator Philip Habib, were ordered to protect the fleeing PLO and provide port security. A massacre by Israeli troops was a possibility acknowledged by the Jerusalem government.

Defeated and reviled by Israeli troops, Christian militias, and Muslims subjected to bogus PLO taxes, Arafat's warriors left in a blaze of gunfire. Trucks full of warriors staged a chattering celebration of automatic weapons. It was designed to mask the third humiliating expulsion for the PLO since 1948. This time they were scattered to reluctant Arab nations forced to accept them by diplomatic pressure. The PLO could celebrate surviving 66,000 artillery shells and two months of endless air attacks on West Beirut by Ariel Sharon. The Israeli minister of defense was watching through a telescope in East Beirut as 1,066 soldiers boarded ships on the first day of the PLO's departure from Beirut harbor on August 22, 1982. The waterfront—West Beirut—was rubble. At least 3,500 Lebanese were dead. Thousands more Lebanese were injured.

"It's a great day for Israel," Sharon told reporters. With the PLO expulsion, Prime Minister Menachem Begin and President Ronald Reagan had achieved the first phase of Sharon's Operation Big Pines. Phase two started the same day. More than 2,000 Syrian troops agreed to retreat from Beirut. Syria's 85th Regiment's troops and tanks completed their withdrawal August 30. That was the Israeli-American's first step in ousting 32,000 of President Hafez al-Assad's soldiers from eastern Lebanon. To Reagan, the PLO and Syria were clients of the Soviet Union. The American president had launched a worldwide attack on governments aided by the Kremlin. Phase three was completed the very next day when Bashir Gemayel, the 34-year-old Phalange warlord, was elected president by the parliament of Lebanon. Israeli occupiers helped produce Gemayel's narrow victory. Camille Chamoun, a Christian leader opposed to Gemayel, changed his mind after a conversation with Begin's adviser Rafael Etian. Chamoun's six votes were ratified with Gemayel's cash. The American president also helped. Ambassador Habib, Reagan's personal representative in the Mideast, spread the word of American support to the Muslim community. Now, Gemayel was in position to approve a peace treaty that would give Israel a trade-rich and dominant position in Lebanon. From the White House in Washington, President Reagan applauded. "The President has noted this morning the election of a new President in Lebanon," his deputy press secretary, Larry Speakes, announced, "and he has sent a message of congratulations to the new President. We also congratulate the Lebanese Parliament in electing the new President through the traditional, constitutional processes during this difficult and trying time."

A week later, President-elect Gemayel was flown to Nahariya, in the north of Israel near the border with Lebanon. Begin was no longer charmed by the young man who wheedled $200 million in Israeli military supplies. Gemayel had already broken a series of solemn promises to Begin and Sharon.

"Where do we stand with the peace treaty?" Begin demanded.

Gemayel began evasively and ended with "A hasty signing of a treaty is not justified, either from a political or security standpoint—"

Begin interrupted. "We believe that the first thing you must do as president is to visit Jerusalem or at least Tel Aviv. Such a visit is of great importance in terms of assuring the people of Israel of your sincerity and desire for normal relations. Isn't that why we went to war and paid the price of hundreds of dead?" The icy, blunt Begin left the president-elect humiliated and angry.

Sharon thought negotiations with Gemayel would still lead to a peace treaty, crown jewel of Operation Big Pines. Other people saw the emergence of an Arab government leader who would likely tolerate Syria's continued occupation of Lebanon rather than a military confrontation. When the Israelis leaked word of Begin's meeting with Gemayel—Gemayel had pleaded for secrecy—the president-elect became testy. Gemayel announced he was severing all ties with Israel. There would be no peace treaty, no visit to Jerusalem and the Knesset. Once again, Bashir Gemayel had betrayed Israel.

Even so, Sharon continued to meet with Gemayel on the future of Palestinians remaining in West Beirut. In talks with US ambassador Morris Draper, who had replaced Habib as Reagan's Mideast representative, Sharon argued 2,500 PLO fighters remained hidden among 200,000 refugees in Sabra, Shatila, and other refugee camps in West Beirut. While some avoided exile, Draper insisted the number was far smaller—only a handful. Once in power, Sharon urged Gemayel to use the Lebanese army—along with Phalange militia—to inspect the camps for fighters and ammunition dumps. Any hint of letting the Phalange into the camps was a recipe for slaughter. Sharon was eyeing the camps, and that worried PLO leader Arafat. He was fearful of Christian attacks on the old men, women, and children the fighters left behind. Arafat insisted the United States guarantee the safety of PLO families in West Beirut. It was spelled out in Article 4 of the agreement Israel, the PLO, and the United States signed: "Law-abiding non-combatant Palestinians who remained in Beirut" would be protected. In addition, Habib—as the president's representative—had repeatedly assured the PLO that Reagan was guaranteeing the protection of PLO families. The document showed the American guarantee was based on support from Israel and the Phalange. That foundation was crumbling with talks between Sharon and Gemayel about cleaning out the camps. Arafat was reassured by the Bersaglieri. The Italians had stowed their feathered helmets, donned the red fez, and set up professional defensive positions just outside the Sabra and Shatila Palestinian refugee camps. Commander Tosetti invaded the poverty-ridden urban warren with Italian food and medical care. Almost daily he was photographed beaming at a different baby in his arms. His boss, Brigadier General Franco Angioni pulled his pistol and broke up a fight between a Phalange thug and a Palestinian. The Italians were heroes in the PLO camps.

Wearing his signature checkered keffiyeh and military green, Arafat seemed relaxed and smiling as leader of the PLO rearguard on August 30 in Beirut harbor. Arafat grinned and waved a branch of an olive tree, a symbol of Mideast peace. The final group of exiles was under the security of the US Marines, commanded by the Scotland-born Lieutenant Colonel Robert Johnston. When the French government sent Ambassador Paul-Marc Henry with a 50-man honor guard to give Arafat a sendoff, Johnston ordered Marine jeeps to block the way.

"This has been agreed with the American ambassador," Henry complained.

"Well, it hasn't been communicated to me," Johnston said. Three of Henry's jeeps pushed by the Marines, and Johnston decided to let them go.

The last of the PLO left the next day. Arriving in Beirut soon after was Defense Secretary Weinberger. Johnston told the defense chief that the Marines' mission was completed. Weinberger favored their departure. Only Habib, now retired and in California, urged extending the stay of the multinational defense force of American, French, and Italian troops. So on September 9 the Marines started to go back to their ships for a return to Naples. The French left next. The Bersaglieri disassembled their defensive position around the Sabra and Shatila refugee camps.

Five days later, the swirl of the Lebanese chaos changed everything. Preparations were made at Phalange headquarters in East Beirut for another Tuesday afternoon speech by President-elect Gemayel. His routine made it easy for Habib Tanious Shartouni, whose sister had a third-floor apartment in the building where Gemayel would speak. They were members of a family with personal ties to the Phalange. Militia guards had no idea Shartouni was secretly a member of the Syrian National Party at war with the Christians. They paid no attention as Shartouni loaded the apartment with high explosives. He detonated the bomb at 4:10 p.m., September 14, with a remote control. That night, two Israeli officers confirmed what the Phalange militia refused to accept—Bashir Gemayel, his faced crushed beyond recognition, was dead in the Hôtel-Dieu de France hospital. The watch on his wrist, a white-gold wedding ring, and notes of congratulations in the pockets of his blue suit were proof. The man Begin, Sharon, and Reagan were betting on to redraw the map of the Levant was a victim of the same sort of violence he lived by.

Gemayel's legacy unfolded the same night, as Begin and Sharon anticipated the course of certain Christian revenge on Sabra and Shatila. Five months later, a commission headed by Yitzhak Kahan, president of the Israeli Supreme Court, shocked the world with grisly details of events between September 14 and 18, 1982. The panel spattered blood from what became known as the Sabra and Shatila massacre on the most senior members of the Israeli government and Israel Defense Forces. Sharon was forced from office, generals were relieved, and courts-martial were ordered. Step by step, the Kahan Commission used evidence and testimony to show Israel's culpability in the killing of between 750 and 2,500 old men, women, children, and infants by knife-wielding members of Gemayel's militia. The panel harked back to the days of pogroms of murder and rape by local hooligans against residents of the European Jewish shtetls.

"The Jewish public's stand has always been that the responsibility for such deeds falls not only on those who rioted and committed the atrocities, but also on those who were responsible for safety and public order, who could have prevented the disturbances and did not fulfill their obligations in this respect," the commission said. Over four months, the panel called 58 witnesses to testify during 60 different sessions. Its staff collected 180 statements from 163 people, including one young Israeli soldier who was on a rooftop monitoring Phalange operations in the camps below. The youth heard women screaming from inside the camps.

"What was that?" he asked. A more senior soldier just laughed at him.

The very night of Gemayel's assassination, Begin, calling it purely a protective measure, gave Sharon permission to enter West Beirut. Sharon alerted commanders and, according to one officer, discussed sending Phalange forces into the PLO camps, which Sharon denied before the Kahan Commission. Israeli tanks seized key West Beirut junctures the next morning. Tanks were lined on both the west and east entrances to the sprawling camps, blocking escape. The same day, Sharon met with Phalange militia leaders, including Elie Hobeika, branded as a "psychopathic killer" by US ambassador Robert Dillon. Sharon stressed the goal of destroying PLO infrastructure remaining in West Beirut and the dangers of terrorists running loose in the city.

"I don't want a single one of them left," Sharon said.

"How do you single them out?" Hobeika asked.

"We'll discuss that at a more restricted session," Sharon said.

The Israel Defense Forces set up a command post on the roof of an abandoned five-story building overlooking Sabra and Shatila. IDF Major General Amir Drori was in command. His deputy was Brigadier General Amos Yaron. The IDF was greeted by gunfire when it secured the camps. An estimated 200 men were firing from PLO positions, but the opposition soon faded. General Rafael Eitan, chief of staff of the IDF, reported to Sharon in Jerusalem at 10 a.m. on Thursday, September 16. Eitan said the camps were surrounded by tanks. All was quiet. If the Phalangists or the Lebanese army were willing to enter, they would be welcome, Eitan told Sharon. Both men knew the Lebanese government refused Lebanese army participation.

"I'd send in the Phalangists," Sharon said.

"They're thirsting for revenge," Eitan said. "There could be torrents of blood."

Later that day, at the main IDF command post overlooking the camps, Hobeika showed up on the rooftop to coordinate Phalange operations with General Drori of the IDF. Drori admonished Hobeika to act properly when he and his 150 men moved through the camps. More than a dozen such warnings were issued by IDF officers on the spot, evidence that they expected the worse from the Phalange.

According to the Kahan report, the United States was warned about the looming slaughter at 5 p.m. when President Reagan's personal emissary showed up for a meeting with Sharon and IDF generals. A month earlier, Israel had made a pledge to the United States never to invade Beirut. "Circumstances changed," Sharon coldly told Ambassador Morris Draper. He had debated with Sharon about remaining PLO fighters and the need to clean out Sabra and Shatila. Now the West Beirut camps were under Israeli control.

"Who will go in? The Lebanese army and security forces?" Draper asked.

"And the Phalange," interjected Major General Yehoshua Saguy.

"Not the Phalange," Draper cried out.

Then Draper got an oral face-slapping from Eitan, the IDF chief of staff. "Lebanon is at the point of exploding into a frenzy of revenge," Eitan told Draper. "No one can stop them. They're obsessed with the idea of revenge. I'm telling you some of their commanders visited me and I could see in their eyes that it's going to be a relentless slaughter." No hint that Eitan and Sharon had surrounded the camps and opened the door to the Phalange.

Draper and US ambassador Samuel Lewis were not told by either Sharon or Eitan of Israel's facilitation of the Phalange's plans. But it was an easy guess for the two veteran US diplomats. As the meeting was ending in Jerusalem, Hobeika's men were slipping into the south and west entrances to Sabra and Shatila. It was getting dark, and PLO defenders began firing rifles at the invaders. The Phalangists' liaison with the IDF, Jesse Soker, showed up at the command post and asked for support. The IDF complied by firing 81 mm mortar flares, turning night into day for the Phalange mayhem. Later, Israeli aircraft dropped flares over the camps. The Phalange were killing men, women, and children, mainly with knives. In some instances, live grenades were hung around individual necks and then exploded. There was one instance of a man in spiked boots crushing an infant to pieces. The Christian cross was carved in the chests of many victims. The Phalange radio net monitored by the IDF recorded one exchange shortly after the militia entered the camps.

"We've rounded up 50 women and children," one of Hobeika's men reported. "What should we do with them?"

"That's the last time you're going to ask me," commander Hobeika replied. "You know what to do."

Another intercept asked what to do with 45 men.

"Do God's will," replied Soker. The Phalange liaison showed up in the IDF mess hall later and boasted 300 people had been killed (he later changed that number to 250). Yaron, the IDF general in charge of the command post, grew increasingly uneasy. Yaron criticized Soker for the civilian killings. Soker promised to do better. But Yaron got a stomach full when his intelligence officer gave him an update on Phalange bloodletting at 8:40 p.m. The Kahan Commission reproduced the report as recorded by the IDF History Department soldiers on the scene.

"One has the impression that the fighting is not particularly serious," the officer told Yaron. "And it seems that they're trying to decide what to do with the people they find inside. On the one hand, there are no terrorists in the camps; Sabra is empty. . . . Apparently, some decision has been made to concentrate them together and they're leading them off somewhere outside the camp. Yet I also heard from Jesse [Soker on the radio], 'Do what your heart tells you because everything comes from God,' meaning I don't—"

Yaron cut him off. He had talked to Soker. "They're not having any problems." The intelligence officer asked Yaron: "And there's no danger to their lives?" They won't harm them, Yaron said. Yaron did not want to believe what an IDF tank officer saw outside the camps. Lieutenant Avi Grabowsky witnessed Phalange militia executing a number of Palestinians from Shatila.

"Why are you killing women and children?" Grabowsky shouted. "Women give birth to children and children grow up into terrorists," a Phalangist shouted back. Four Christian militias repeatedly raped a young woman who entered the camps Friday to visit her mother.

As the massacre was under way Friday, the Israeli cabinet was still meeting at 9 p.m. General Eitan informed them the Phalange were operating in the camps but under control of watching IDF officers. The IDF chief of staff's effort to minimize events was instantly ridiculed by David Levy, a Moroccan-born Jew who led an increasingly large bloc of Sephardi voters. Perhaps because of his origin, elite Israelis ridiculed Levy as stupid, so stupid that those Polish jokes became David Levy jokes in Israel. But he showed instant recognition that Israel and the world would not tolerate the IDF's role as handmaiden to a calculated slaughter, that no one would believe Israel's intention had been to go in to create order and that whatever explanations it gave for what ensued would not stand up.

It did not stand up with the population of Israel, where many serve in the armed forces from youth to middle age. The IDF was a source of national pride. Shock and disbelief greeted news reports that swiftly circulated on Rosh Hashanah, the Jewish New Year, on Sunday, September 19. The massacre at Sabra and Shatila had continued until General Yaron ordered the Phalange out by 6 a.m. Saturday, September 18. Within hours, the streets were flooded with reporters, photographers, and film crews, documenting the nightmare: mounds of bodies, an alleyway where a dozen men were lined up and gunned down, scattered corpses of small children and infants, a woman who had been stripped and disemboweled, and overpowering everything a stench that was too much for some. Odd Karsten Tveit, a Norwegian reporter, walked through narrating the scene to a tape recorder for later broadcast. Every few feet, Tveit would pause to vomit, then resume his narration. And then vomit again. Israel supplied a bulldozer—once IDF markings were removed—and trucked out some of the dead.

News dispatches, photographs, and network film produced a global shock. Interviews with IDF troops still surrounding the camps Sunday underlined Israeli government involvement with the Phalange massacre. The Israeli government later that day acknowledged "coordination" but said events got out of control. At one cabinet meeting, Prime Minister Begin predicted a short-lived furor. "*Goyim* killing *goyim*," Begin said dismissively—non-Jews killing each other. His phrase was widely quoted.

Ze'ev Schiff, a brilliant reporter for the daily national newspaper *Haaretz*, sensed a sea change. "Something snapped in Israel over that holiday weekend . . . ," he wrote later. "The war had not crowned their country with a great political and military victory but had dragged it down to the sordid depths of the Lebanese maelstrom and stained its honor indelibly. . . . The government and army were implicated in the commission of atrocities. Sabra and Shatila had become synonymous with infamy." A week later, 400,000 Israelis took to the streets of Tel Aviv to demand the resignations of Begin and Sharon. SHAME, read a large banner. That a tenth of the population would show up to protest led to the organization of the Kahan Commission.

Begin continued to defend Sharon. The prime minister rejected the panel's February 8, 1993, call to remove Sharon as minister of defense. The issue was debated at a crucial cabinet meeting February 10 as thousands of Israelis demonstrated outside. A large part of the crowd was calling for Sharon's ouster. It included Peace Now activist Emil Grunzweig, a Romanian-born immigrant. Another part of the crowd was cheering for Sharon. "Arik, King of Israel," they shouted. A hand grenade tossed into the crowd exploded and killed Grunzweig. Shortly thereafter the cabinet voted 16–1 to remove the minister of defense.

Despite Kahan's indictment, Begin kept *mon general* as a minister without portfolio. The divided crowd yelling for and against Sharon reflected a split in Israeli society that has only deepened with changing immigration patterns and attitudes. Fading fast were General Moshe Dayan's appeals to understand the plight of Palestinians. "Before their eyes we turn into our homestead the land and villages in which they and their forefathers have lived . . . ," the hero of the 1967 war wrote. "Let us not be afraid to see the hatred that accompanies and consumes the lives of hundreds of thousands of Arabs who sit all around us and await the moment when their hand will be able to reach our blood."

To Begin and Sharon, that Arab hatred deserved refugee camps and death. The Polish immigrant had turned Palestinians into the new Nazis who deserved the worst because they threatened Jews. The extreme attitude was adopted by Rabbi Meir Kahane, a founder of the Jewish Defense League. Kahane launched his campaign for parliament in the midst of the Israeli invasion of Lebanon and would eventually run commercials with blood dripping down ancient steps. Arab blood for sure. For Begin, Sabra and Shatila was an extension of the founding fathers' fight for the land of Israel.

Near Jerusalem, the Muslim village of Deir Yassin came under attack on April 9, 1948, by Jewish paramilitary forces, including the Irgun. Houses were blown up with people inside, and other villagers were shot: 107, including women and children, were killed. The survivors were loaded on trucks that were driven through Jerusalem in a victory parade. (The village was later annexed to the new state

of Israel.) On April 10, Albert Einstein, the celebrated physicist, re-
volted by the massacre, ended his support for American Friends of
the Fighters for the Freedom of Israel. A *New York Times* op-ed
reviling the Deir Yassin massacre was published December 2, signed
by many prominent American Jews.

In their article, they singled out Irgun leader Menachem Begin.

7

Going for Broke

In observance of Rosh Hashanah, President Ronald Reagan recalled the Jewish New Year's Day legend of sorting the righteous from the wicked. "The wholly righteous are at once inscribed and sealed in the Book of Life," Reagan said. "The wholly wicked are at once inscribed and sealed in the Book of Death." His previously prepared statement was issued September 18 as newspaper dispatches and network film unveiled the horrors of Sabra and Shatila. The massacre jolted Reagan. And the shock disabled his top advisers. William Clark, his adviser on national security affairs, and Secretary of State George Shultz filled the aging actor with misinformation. They could not sort the righteous from the wicked.

At a September 17 political fund-raiser in New Jersey, Reagan seemed to justify Israel's invasion of West Beirut. "It is true that what led them to move back in was the attack—after the assassination of the elected President there—the attack on his forces by some of the leftist militia that are still there in West Beirut," Reagan said in off-the-cuff remarks. There was no such attack on Israeli forces.

In Jerusalem, Ambassador Morris Draper, the president's Mideast representative, was in a rage at the unjustified incursion and demanding an Israeli withdrawal. Reagan's diary for September 18, 1982, showed him parroting the cover story issued by the Phalangists to hide their murderous rampage. The state-run *Voice of Lebanon* reported a Phalange statement at 6:30 p.m. It blamed the massacre on the forces of Major Saad Haddad, who controlled a buffer zone between southern Lebanon and Israel. Haddad, a Greek Catholic detested by the Maronite Christians, was financed and controlled by Israel. At the same time, the Phalange denied any involvement in Sabra and Shatila. The statement was dismissed in Jerusalem and Beirut as a bogus and feeble cover-up attempt by the blood-soaked Christian militia. Washington perceived it differently. Based on official information Saturday, September 18, Reagan wrote in his diary: "In Beirut, Haddad's Christian Phalangist Militia entered a Palestine refugee camp and massacred men, women and children. The Israelis did nothing to halt it."

The next day during a National Security Council crisis meeting, Reagan still had not grasped Israel's role as a facilitator of the Phalange invasion of the camps. "The Israelis did finally attempt to oust the killers," Reagan wrote in his diary. "They have proclaimed their outrage." Reagan may have been defending Israel so as to defend his support for Jerusalem's invasion of Lebanon and backing of the Phalange leadership.

Getting their story straight took on more importance as Reagan braced for political criticism of American failures that contributed to the massacre. PLO leader Yasser Arafat spelled it out at a news conference: "I ask Italy, France and the United States: What of your promise to protect the inhabitants of Beirut?" That sort of second-guessing stung some in Washington. "The guilt feeling affected us all," said Army General John Vessey, Chairman of the Joint Chiefs of Staff. Defense Secretary Caspar Weinberger had no such qualms. "I don't think there's any connection," he said when asked about the withdrawal of the multinational force 10 days before the massacre. Philip Habib saw it differently. "The Italian force was right outside those camps," he said. He had retired—for a second time— earlier that summer after a star-studded career as an ambassador, troubleshooter, and, until his heart gave out, undersecretary of state for political affairs—the number-two post at the State Department. Reagan had summoned him out of retirement to struggle with Israel and Lebanon as his personal representative. Habib's parents were Maronite Christian immigrants to Brooklyn, the same religion embraced by Bashir Gemayel. It did not help him avoid the bumps, bruises, and bloody noses of the diplomatic minefield that was Israel, Syria, and Lebanon. At least three of his cease-fire agreements vanished in Israeli intransigence. Begin manipulated and Sharon lied. Their willingness to brush off Habib, who carried the implied threat of presidential retribution, reflected confidence in bipartisan support for Israel from 435 US congressional districts. Regardless of Reagan's—or Habib's— threats and demands, Begin counted on Congress for an uninterrupted flow of weapons and billions in financial aid.

Habib went home September 1 to huzzahs and the Presidential Medal of Freedom, the highest civilian award, at a White House ceremony. His crowning achievement in Beirut—the peaceful removal of Arafat and his PLO army—was soon awash in Palestinian blood. In an interview at his retirement home in San Francisco, he explained how Bashir Gemayel and Sharon pledged to Habib that no harm would befall Sabra, Shatila, and other refugee camps in West Beirut. It was a thin reed at best. The duplicitous Gemayel was plotting a "cleanout" of the camps with Sharon before he was killed. "Sharon was a killer, obsessed by hatred of the Palestinians," Habib said. "I had given Arafat an undertaking that his people would not be harmed, but this was totally disregarded by Sharon, whose word was worth nothing." Palestinian old men, women, children, and infants paid the price.

As a result, American influence was at a low ebb when Reagan faced a news conference September 28. It was preceded by Jeane Kirkpatrick, US ambassador to the United Nations, saying the American government shared responsibility for the Beirut massacre, which made Reagan squirm. Helen Thomas of United Press International got right to it.

"Mr. President," she asked, "when the Palestinian fighters were forced to leave Beirut, they said that they had America's word of honor that those they left behind would not be harmed. Now comes U.N. Ambassador Jeane Kirkpatrick, who says that America must share in the blame for these massacres. My question to you is, do you agree with that judgment?"

Reagan slid his answer to responsibility for withdrawal of the multinational force, not the protection of PLO families Thomas asked about: "I don't think that specifically there could be assigned as a responsibility on our part for withdrawing our troops. They were sent in there with one understanding. They were there to oversee and make sure that the PLO left Lebanon. That mission was completed, virtually without incident, and they left. Then, who could have foreseen the assassination of the President-elect that led to the other violence and so forth."

Reagan sought to sideline criticism over a premature withdrawal of the multinational force by redeploying American, French, and Italian troops back to Beirut. Although this decision was fraught with consequences, Reagan rushed it through the day after learning of the massacre. He described a September 19 National Security Council meeting in his diary.

"I finally told our group we should go for broke," Reagan wrote. "Let's tell the people we are in at the request of the Lebanese— sending the multi-national force back in. Italy has agreed and we believe the French will, too. We are asking the Israelis to leave Beirut. We are asking Arabs to intervene and persuade Syrians to leave Lebanon. . . . No more half way gestures, clear the whole situation while the [multinational force] is on hand to assure order. . . . The wheels are now in motion."

Reagan's yee-hah tone belied an intense debate over sending too small a force to deal with too big a threat. Perhaps the baseline for such a military commitment was drawn in 1958 by a former five-star Army general, President Dwight D. Eisenhower. When instability and a possible war between Christians and Muslims threatened Lebanon during the Cold War, Eisenhower sent 14,000, a division. Ike instantly outgunned all comers. American troops occupied Beirut for three months.

This time, there were 30,000 Israel Defense Forces troops and armor surrounding Beirut. Syria still had 35,000 troops in Lebanon. In addition to the Christian militas, their ancient Muslim enemy, the Druse, had a well-armed force of 8,000 in the Shuf Mountains overlooking Beirut, and oddball militias with Kalashnikovs set up checkpoints all over the city. Shiites, the poverty-stricken Muslims of the southern suburbs, were being organized into a force called the Amal. Wall posters throughout the Shia neighborhoods showed the image of the Ayatollah Ruhollah Khomeini, the leader of Iran's "Death to America" campaign. Iran was joining the Lebanese stew in 1982.

Reagan's National Security Council staff urged him to act like the leader of a superpower instead of putting a multinational force of about 5,000 on the ground. "There were those of us saying that if we're going to do anything at all, now's the time to be bold," said Geoffrey Kemp, a senior staff member. Three American divisions and two French divisions, enough to make up a full-blown armored infantry corps! Not to mention as many as three aircraft carriers and cannon on warships off Beirut harbor. That would be enough brute power, Kemp said, to issue "ultimata to the Israelis and the Syrians to get their forces out of Lebanon." No simpering requests.

Reagan liked Kemp's idea. Defense Secretary Weinberger was unalterably opposed. Overruling Weinberger would mean firing one of the oldest members of the Reagan team. The president had no stomach for it. Instead he opted for resending the same 5,000-man force, including about 1,200 US Marines, a celebrated light infantry unit. He announced his decision two days later, and it became an instant political debate. Under the War Powers Act, the Democratic Congress could demand US withdrawal if the Marines came under attack. House Speaker Tip O'Neill quickly raised the issue after Reagan's September 20 announcement. It was raised again at the September 28 White House news conference.

Q: Mr. President, do you have a plan for getting the United States out of Lebanon if fighting should break out there, or could the Marine presence there lead to another long entanglement such as Vietnam?

The President: No, I don't see anything of that kind taking place there at all. And the Marines are going in there, into a situation with a definite understanding as to what we're supposed to do. I believe that we are going to be successful in seeing the other foreign forces leave Lebanon. And then [at] such time as Lebanon says that they have the situation well in hand, why, we'll depart.

Q: Sir, if fighting should break out again, would you pull the marines out?

The President: You're asking a hypothetical question, and I've found out that I never get in trouble if I don't answer one of those. . . .

Q: Mr. President, you've told us that you're sending marines to Lebanon for a limited amount of time, and yet you haven't told us what the limit is. Can you give us a general idea of how long you expect them to stay there and tell us precisely what you would like to see them accomplish before they withdraw?

The President: I can't tell you what the time element would be. I can tell you what it is that they should accomplish, and I hope sooner rather than later. One, they're there along with our allies, the French and the Italians, to give a kind of support and stability while the Lebanese Government seeks to reunite its people. And during this time, while that's taking place, the withdrawal, as quickly as possible, to their own borders of the Israelis and the Syrians. Now, there we've had declarations from both countries that they want to do that. So, I am reasonably optimistic about that.

Q: Are you then saying that they will remain there until all foreign forces are withdrawn?

The President: Yes, because I think that's going to come rapidly; I think we're going to see the withdrawal.

Reagan's optimism was based on the intuition of the most illustrious star in the Republican firmament: George Pratt Shultz, 61, an economist, a professor, a business school dean, a member of the President's Council of Economic Advisers, a secretary of labor, a director of management and budget, a secretary of the treasury, and president of Bechtel, one of the world's largest engineering companies. He had an easy manner of a man who worked with students. "That's Shultz with an *h,*" he said as I wrote down his name for the first time in 1968. "I had to keep reminding the Marines of that." He had survived the carnage of the South Pacific as a Marine company commander. It taught him to survive untainted for eight years under President Richard Nixon and the Watergate scandal. Two cabinet colleagues wound up in orange jumpsuits in federal prison. But as Reagan's new secretary of state, Shultz had stepped on the shifting ground of Israel, Syria, and Lebanon.

"George Shultz, God bless his soul, didn't know shit from Shinola about the Middle East," said Alexander Haig, his predecessor.

Because of Bechtel's global projects, Shultz got to know the Kingdom of Saudi Arabia quite well. Multimillion-dollar projects in the oil-rich desert nation led Bechtel to be an important supporter of Riyadh in Congress. As the corporation's president, Shultz oversaw Bechtel's support of the Saudis in the fight for US airborne warning and control (AWAC) jets. Reagan prevailed over intense Israeli opposition in selling the US Air Force planes to Riyadh. In State Department patois, Shultz would be considered an Arabist when it came to Mideast policy. The Arabists were not predisposed to Israel like Reagan and Haig.

Reagan's first splashy Mideast initiative authored by Shultz had a pro-Arab, anti-Israel flavor. Announced the day after PLO leader Yasser Arafat departed Beirut, Reagan called it a "fresh start" for the Mideast peace process that had stalled with the departure of President Jimmy Carter. It would create a Palestinian homeland on the West Bank and in Gaza that would be supervised by King

Hussein of Jordan. There would be a total freeze on new Israeli settlements. Menachem Begin was the first Israeli prime minister to proclaim the West Bank—seized from Jordan in the 1967 war—as ancient Judea and Samaria, part of the Kingdom of Israel that had fallen in 721 BC. The land was the foundation for the future of the greater Land of Israel, "Eretz Israel." Begin rejected the plan when it was previewed to him before Reagan's public announcement. So did Arafat, the key beneficiary of Shultz's largesse.

The "fresh start" vanished in the aftermath of the Sabra and Shatila massacre.

8

A Path to Glory

The man with the most profound effect on Ronald Reagan's diplomatic legacy was known to some—jealous contemporaries, for instance—as a broke-dick light colonel. Washington was full of them: hardworking, dedicated lieutenant colonels or Navy commanders with 20 years or more on duty who were passed over for promotion. Some had good explanations for the career-ending rejection. Not all were inferior human beings. Marine Lieutenant Colonel Robert Carl "Bud" McFarlane simply resigned his commission. He had sold his soul to Henry Kissinger, adviser on national security affairs to Presidents Richard Nixon and Gerald Ford. By extending his tour as a military aide at the rarified altitude of the White House, McFarlane knew, he was damaging his Marine Corps career. Regular officers sneered at men who left the front line to become slaves to the powerful. They were referred to as "horse holders," patiently holding the bridle, brushing away flies while waiting on political appointees who were often ignorant and a bit corrupt. Military aides arrived before dawn and left after midnight. They sacrificed their home life so that their superiors could enjoy a lighter workload. Arriving political bosses found mail opened and answered. Phone calls were returned and lunch schedules were set. Aides knew the hidden location of the White House Map Room. No job was beneath them. Flattery was endless. Bosses were deeply grateful. Doors were opened. Army Lieutenant Colonel Alexander Haig and, eventually, his deputy, Army Major George Joulwan, both rose from the rancor of the Nixon White House to be four-star generals and Supreme Allied Commander in Europe. And Nixon's gratitude would transform Haig into secretary of state under President Reagan.

No military aide on Kissinger's staff worked harder than McFarlane. On a Nixon vacation to San Clemente, California, McFarlane got off Air Force One, went directly to the offices of the Coast Guard station, and worked nonstop through the entire vacation. "I worked 85 hours a week or more, seven days a week and only saw my children when they got up to have breakfast with me at 5 o'clock," McFarlane said. But it was a path to glory. McFarlane would parlay his years as a grinder for Kissinger into his image as a foreign policy mastermind who executed Reagan's most fateful decisions. McFarlane easily outshone superiors who, like Reagan, were disinterested in foreign affairs, never grasped crucial facts, and failed to comprehend events that exploded before their eyes. McFarlane became captain on a ship of foreign policy fools. He was the proverbial one-eyed man in the Land of the Blind. In 1982, McFarlane was made the number-two man on Reagan's National Security Council. In 1983, he was promoted to be Reagan's special representative to the Mideast as US Marines were redeployed as part of Beirut's multinational force. Before the end of that year, he became adviser on national security affairs to the president of the United States—the same post his idol, Henry

Kissinger, had held. McFarlane now had his own platoon of military aides.

McFarlane loved Kissinger and the levers of power. For White House reporters, Bud McFarlane would perform a spot-on imitation of the gravelly baritone with the heavy German accent. Eventually, McFarlane came to believe he could orchestrate world-changing foreign policy, as did Nixon—and Kissinger—in restoring diplomatic relations with the People's Republic of China. Men and women who served Washington's powerful sometimes cast themselves in their boss's role. *Why not me?* The syndrome had been identified as Potomac Fever. The fever would one day bring McFarlane close to death.

McFarlane attended the Naval Academy at Annapolis, Maryland. In his third year, he had misgivings about becoming a professional killer. What about the ministry? That was slapped out of him by his father, William McFarlane, an overbearing former Texas congressmen who left Bud with a lifelong inability to smile. "Look, you're going to be a naval officer, so study hard, graduate, learn your Navy skills. That's your job," he admonished his son. McFarlane became a Marine warrior. As a captain commanding the Foxtrot Battery of the 12th Marines' 2nd Battalion, McFarlane became one of the first combat troops in South Vietnam. Two Marine battalions landed on March 8, 1965, ostensibly to provide security for Danang Airbase, which had come under attack by the Viet Cong. Until that attack, the 25,000 US military already in Vietnam were primarily noncombatants—advisers to the South Vietnamese army. After the Marines waded ashore, Vietnamese girls draped flowers over their necks. Some held signs: WELCOME GALLANT MARINES. This American combat force would mushroom to more than 500,000 three years later.

After his first tour in Vietnam, McFarlane entered the world of diplomatic nuance. For two years, he attended the Graduate School of International Studies in Geneva, a center for global diplomacy. After a second combat tour, McFarlane brought his Geneva credentials along to the Nixon White House in 1972.

In the jungles of Vietnam, McFarlane saw the start of the American conflict that killed up to 2 million Vietnamese, North and South. Fate also placed McFarlane in the middle of final American withdrawal ten years later. As a military aide in 1975 to Kissinger—then secretary of state—Major McFarlane manned the communication link between the White House and the US embassy in Saigon. The ambassador, Graham Martin, was racked with pneumonia and trying to evacuate US-employed Vietnamese. Panic swept Saigon. Gunfire had killed two Marines on the embassy security staff. North Vietnamese troops had seized the city. Martin balked when ordered to halt the evacuation to warships standing offshore. President Gerald Ford and Kissinger lost patience. Kissinger told McFarlane to tell Martin to board the last rooftop helicopter—now. When Martin demanded more time, McFarlane dropped the formality and cut him off. "Graham, you have your orders," McFarlane said.

McFarlane's nine-year tour in the Nixon and Ford years as a slavish military aide led directly led to his climb to the highest reaches of US national security in the Reagan administration. Operating in the shadow of Kissinger gave McFarlane a grasp of foreign policy and an insider's knowledge of the complex national security establishment. However, while McFarlane could imitate and emulate his famous mentor, he lacked the depth, breadth, and foresight of Henry Kissinger. As a professor at Harvard, Kissinger was immersed in global machinations for 20 years before joining government.

Kissinger's brilliance was instantly embraced by the hardcore civil servants who actually ran national security in the State and Defense Departments, the Senate, and the Central Intelligence Agency. Kissinger was the implementer of Richard Nixon's obsession for world affairs that dated back to his eight years as Eisenhower's vice president. McFarlane lacked Kissinger's résumé and intellect, as well as the charm and wit that Kissinger used to win friends and disarm opponents. By contrast, McFarlane was almost without humor—even smiles. He used two-dollar words and dropped his voice to impress. With strangers, he gave off an air of insincerity. When the Republicans lost the White House in 1976, McFarlane fled to the staff of Senator John Tower, a senior member of the Senate Armed Services Committee. It was a haven for passed-over lieutenant colonels.

When Reagan became president-elect in 1980, McFarlane was certain of returning to the White House. Instead, he was blackballed by Richard Vincent Allen, a California conservative Reagan picked to be adviser on national security affairs. Allen, from the Hoover Institution at Stanford University, had served as Reagan's foreign policy expert for three years, including the presidential campaign against Jimmy Carter. It was just before the 1980 vote and Reagan was rattled over the possibility of some "October surprise" from the Carter White House. As Allen recalls it, McFarlane phoned saying Senator Tower had someone Allen should meet. The meeting was arranged at the L'Enfant Plaza Hotel.

"There's McFarlane with this big fat Iranian guy who tells us that he is connected to the Shah's son and how he has all this influence and he can get the hostages back," Allen recalled. The hostages from the US embassy in Tehran who had been held for almost a year were a symbol of Carter's weakness. The meeting angered Allen. "I said,

'Buddy, I don't know who you are, but we've only got one president. Don't talk to me about getting the hostages back.'"

Allen was equally incensed by McFarlane. "This had dynamite all over it," Allen said. "I could have killed him for the bad judgment that he showed." With only a few days to go, Allen saw McFarlane meddling in an issue that could explode in Reagan's face. Using Iranian connections to free American hostages was an issue destined to haunt McFarlane and Reagan years later. McFarlane represented the bad judgment and clumsiness of some military men with foreign policy ambitions. Allen had a distaste for military aides angling for careers at the White House. Army, Air Force, Navy, Marines—they all acted as spies for their military superiors. Allen once caught a Navy yeoman faxing secret Nixon documents to Admiral Thomas Moorer, then chairman of the Joint Chiefs. One year and out was Allen's rule for horse holders.

When Allen slammed shut the door to the White House, McFarlane found another entrance into the administration. It came from the most successful horse holder in White House history—Secretary of State Alexander Meigs Haig. With Richard Nixon's intervention, Haig won the biggest plum Reagan had to offer. As president, Nixon paid particular attention to the governor of California. More than one foreign assignment as goodwill ambassador was given to Reagan. Friends take care of friends. Haig shared duties with McFarlane on the Kissinger staff at the Nixon White House, having asked him to be counselor to the State Department. There he found the untutored Reagan chum William Clark, now deputy secretary of state. Haig prized the Californian Clark for his Reagan connection. In a year, Richard Allen was out as boss of the National Security Council. Clark quickly returned to Reagan's side at the White

House and replaced Allen. Clark recruited McFarlane as deputy national security adviser to the president of the United States.

Suddenly astounding access to presidential power lay before him. McFarlane tutored Clark at the State Department and would continue at the White House. Clark's ties to Reagan's California team meant National Security Council policy recommendations—McFarlane's ideas—would arrive almost untouched on the president's desk. McFarlane would have a chance to control some portion of American foreign policy. This was confirmed at his first senior staff meeting with Reagan in February of 1982. Someone noted the absence of a coherent Reagan foreign policy. "You don't have one," Reagan was told.

"But you do have a foreign policy, Mr. President," interjected McFarlane. All eyes turned to this veteran of the Nixon White House and the wisdom of Henry Kissinger.

"It has five components," McFarlane said. He ticked off strengthening the country's economic base—essential to underwriting the US foreign aid program; restoring defense; restoring the strength of global alliances; advancing the Mideast peace process by mediating between Israel and her Arab neighbors; and fostering accelerated growth in developing countries. The list wowed Mike Deaver, Reagan's public affairs adviser. He wanted McFarlane to put the five elements on 3" × 5" cards for Reagan's use.

Once McFarlane was out of the safety of his White House office, his lack of qualifications reinforced his lifelong self-doubts. When he was elevated to be Reagan's personal representative in the Mideast, he replaced one of the State Department's most distinguished diplomats. Pin-striped with flowing white hair, the towering Morris Draper was fluent in Arabic and French and could get by in a list of other languages. A University of California Phi Beta Kappa, Draper later studied at the American University of Beirut. He had served in Saudi Arabia, Jordan, and Turkey and was the department's overseer for Jordan, Syria, Iraq, and Lebanon. Draper was skilled at transforming Washington's political decisions into workable diplomacy. He was deputy to superstar ambassador Philip Habib throughout the turmoil of Israel's invasion of Lebanon.

"He was able to deal with the needs of senior policymakers as well as the realities of the world," said Harold Saunders, an assistant secretary of state for President Jimmy Carter. "He really knows the Lebanese situation better than anyone I know in the US Government."

McFarlane was of a different milieu. The US military establishment viewed most global problems as protruding nails that could be settled with the whack of a 12-pound sledge. His first two months of diplomacy, bouncing between Jerusalem, Beirut, and Damascus, were depressing. Reagan's top priority—withdrawal of Israeli and Syrian troops from Lebanon—drew disdain. McFarlane felt Prime Minister Begin dismissed him as an ineffective messenger boy. In Damascus, Syrian president Assad talked for hours, but mostly about topics found in supermarket tabloids. What, for example, was McFarlane's take on the Bermuda Triangle? In Beirut, President Amin Gemayel heard him out. Then, in a confidential tone, Gemayel said:

"You know, Bud, it is hopeless, this thing you are trying to do here."

9

The Party of God

There was a time when everyone came to Baalbek and its fabulous
Roman ruins. The guest book at the Palmyra Hotel showed the signatures of Franklin Delano Roosevelt, Winston Churchill, and Charles
de Gaulle, all dated before World War II. A French count left an
extravagant signature below his claim of being heir to a family that
made France great. A few pages later, a Kuwaiti prince gave the sense
that he was part of the royal family who ruined Kuwait. The ancient
Lebanese city between Beirut and Damascus was on the Grand Tour.
They came for the monuments, for the Great Rift Valley scallions, rad-
ishes, and nuts spread over pink tablecloths, for perfectly grilled spring
chicken with a crimson wine, for the jazz festivals on the steps on the
Temple of Bacchus and for some of the Bekaa Valley's famous hashish.

All these attractions began to fade in the summer of 1982. Hafez
el-Assad, president of Syria, had controlled the city since 1976.
Some of his 35,000 Syrian troops in Lebanon bivouacked in Baalbek. You could see the Lebanese resentment. Waiters at a wedding
party spit as they passed behind the groom, a Syrian captain. Things

got worse with the arrival in July 1982 of the Iranian Revolutionary Guards. Tehran's Islamic Shiite strictures ruined the ambience of the ancient town. The Guards took over the four-star al-Khayyam Hotel and renamed a floor the Ayatollah Khomeini Hospital. Ayatollah Ruhollah Khomeini had transformed a pro-Western Iran with a Shiite Islamic revolution in 1978–79; in the US presidential election year of 1980, revolutionaries seized the American staff at the US embassy in Tehran. The fate of the hostages undermined President Jimmy Carter and boosted chances for Ronald Reagan. Now, President Reagan's intelligence community was almost totally unaware of Baalbek's new frontline role in attacking the United States. Years later, the RAND Corporation and other think tanks would highlight Beirut during seminars such as "The Challenge for Democracies Facing Asymmetric Conflicts." Behind the gobbledygook was a basic question: How do zealots on a shoestring budget humiliate the world's most powerful nation?

One answer was in Baalbek in the spring of 1982, where the tourist and drug trades died in the face of Iranian standards of morality. "Death to America" posters were pasted everywhere.

Until 1982, Assad refused any Iranian presence in Lebanon. Assad lifted the tollgate for Iran in July after Israel used American warplanes and technology to destroy 85 Syrian warplanes in two days. The loss of his air force was not only a national humiliation for a Soviet-trained jet fighter pilot who commanded the Syrian air force before becoming president, but also a personal wound. Syria welcomed the elite Iranian soldiers determined to kill Americans. They papered the ruins as well as the police station with posters of Iran's spiritual leader, the black-turbaned Ayatollah Khomeini.

The Iranians set up in the Sheikh Abdullah barracks in Baalbek. They were soon joined by the Party of God, Beirut Shiite Muslims organized and financed by Iran. Shiites in Lebanon were poor and conservative. They were dominated by Sunni Muslims, who were more moderate in religious beliefs, wealthy, and in political control. With Iran's backing, the Beirut Shiites became the foundation of Hezbollah, which one day would dominate Lebanese politics and become a formidable opponent of Israel.

A tall, slim, and handsome college engineering student arrived in Baalbek that summer of 1982. Nineteen-year-old Imad Fayez Mughniyeh took the number-two spot in Hezbollah and became the liaison with the Guards. He was from the southern Lebanon town of Tyre and had served in the Palestine Liberation Organization and the Amal, the more moderate Shiite militia in his home region. He attended the American University of Beirut, headed by Acting President David Dodge, probably the second most prestigious American post after the US ambassador. On July 19, 1982, Mughniyeh helped stage the kidnapping of Dodge, who was knocked unconscious and bundled into a car in Beirut. Taken to Baalbek by the Hezbollah leader, Dodge was turned over to the Iranian Guards, who later shipped him to Tehran. As a news event, the kidnapping was lost in the midst of Israel's bombardment of Beirut. Dodge's release was the result of negotiations between Secretary of State George Shultz and Syrian president Assad.

In the spring of 1983, Tehran gave the Baalbek crew a bigger target. The Guards provided explosives, the detonators, and the technology. Mughniyeh provided the Beirut end of the operation: the old van, the driver, the inside informant. To enhance the explosion, bottles of butane gas—easily available for cooking, and pioneered as a bomb enhancer by the Irish Republican Army—were mixed in on the floor of the van with 2,000 pounds of high explosive of a type known to be produced in Iran.

The overloaded van pulled up near the US embassy that overlooked

Beirut's glorious corniche and the blue Mediterranean. A Syrian army officer wired the explosives to the detonator in the driver's hands. In the bright sunshine on April 18, the van driver waited for a signal from inside the embassy that American ambassador Robert Dillon had returned from running the three-mile outdoor track at the American University of Beirut.

With the signal, the van driver gunned his engine. The van splintered the single-pole Lebanese police barricade and roared past US Marine guards, up the steps and into the entrance of the seven-story concrete structure. When the driver embraced Allah and his reward of seven virgins, the building pancaked into rubble.

In the ambassador's top-floor office, a sweaty Dillon was struggling out of a Marine T-shirt. He recalled the moment:

All of a sudden, the window blew in. I was very lucky, because I had my arm and the T-shirt in front of my face, which protected me from the flying glass. I ended up flat on my back. I never heard the explosion. Others said that it was the loudest explosion they ever heard. It was heard from a long distance away.

As I lay on the floor on my back, the brick wall behind my desk blew out. Everything seemed to happen in slow motion. The wall fell on my legs; I could not feel them. I thought they were gone. The office filled with smoke, dust, and tear gas. What happened was that the blast first blew in the window and then traveled up an air shaft from the first floor to behind my desk. We had had tear gas canisters on the first floor. The blast set them off so that the air rush that came up through the shaft brought the tear gas with it and also collapsed the wall.

We didn't know what had happened. The central stairway was gone, but the building had another stairway, which we used to make our way down, picking our way through the rubble. We were astounded to see the damage below us. I didn't realize that the entire bay of the building below my office had been destroyed. I hadn't grasped that yet. I remember speculating that some people had undoubtedly been hurt. As we descended, we saw people hurt. Everybody had this funny white look because they were all covered with dust. They were staggering around.

We got to the second floor, still not fully cognizant of how bad it was, although I recognized that major damage had been done. With each second, the magnitude of the explosion became clearer. I saw Marylee [McIntyre] standing; she couldn't see because her face had been cut and her eyes were full of blood. I picked her up and took her over to a window and gave her to someone.

The bombing killed 63, including 17 Americans. That included most of the Mideast leadership of the Central Intelligence Agency, who were in Beirut for a conference. The body of the CIA Beirut bureau chief dangled from the upper floors of the wreckage. The regional boss, Robert Ames, a CIA superstar, was also dead. The embassy overlooked Beirut harbor, and Ames's hand was found floating there. It was identified by his wedding ring.

Reagan told reporters it was "a vicious terrorist bombing." But the prevailing Washington view was one of surprise and confusion. Army General John Vessey, chairman of the Joint Chiefs of Staff, was consternated, saying in retrospect, "Although it was a great tragedy, it seemed like an inexplicable aberration." Not so in the Arab world still seething over American support for Israel's invasion of Lebanon and the 56-day siege of Beirut. There, the US embassy bombing was very pertinent revenge.

CIA outrage led to a particularly ruthless investigation that resulted in the firing of an agency officer who participated in the beatings of four suspects. They did not make a Baalbek connection. That came from combing through routine intercepts by the US National Security Agency of Tehran radio traffic with Damascus. In the spring of 1983 SIGINT—signal intelligence—snatched from the ether a message from Tehran to its embassy in Damascus: Permission to carry out the operation and $25,000 will be transferred to the embassy. No target, no date, no type of attack. What could it mean? Perhaps the attack was orchestrated by Syrian president Assad. Damascus's vigorous denial brought into focus the Iranian Revolutionary Guards in Baalbek—and a new, hard-nosed Shiite militia called Hezbollah.

For Imad Mughniyeh, destruction of the embassy was the start of a career that would lead to the FBI's Most Wanted List and a global reputation as a killer of the most Americans until Osama bin Laden's 2001 attack on the World Trade Center.

Only a handful of American experts understood the depth of the threat being mounted in the ancient tourist town in the Bekaa Valley. One was William Corbett, an Army Special Forces colonel and security expert dispatched to Beirut for an assessment from US Army European headquarters in Stuttgart, Germany. He dismissed as "nonsensical" the perception that the embassy bombing was a random act. Terrorist organizations such as Hezbollah have long-range goals.

"More applicable," Colonel Corbett warned his superiors in Stuttgart, "would be a series of terrorist acts, each, if possible, more spectacular and costly than the previous. U.S. military forces represent the most defined and logical terrorist target."

It was one of many clear warnings that never made it to the commander of the lightly defended US Marine force at Beirut International Airport.

10

Peace in a Madhouse

Colonel Timothy Geraghty waved away his aide.

The Marine commander was too busy for a phone call on September 8, 1983. He was in a crisis meeting at the Beirut Ministry of Defense. Whistling artillery and mortar rounds exploded nearby. His Marines in Lebanon—Task Force 62—had come under fire once again. Two had been killed last night for a total of four, along with 29 wounded, in the past week. Geraghty's Atlantic Fleet commander, a three-star general, was in from Norfolk, Virginia. His division commander from Camp Lejeune, North Carolina, a two-star, was also at the table. Their earlier inspection of the Marine front line was cut short by a spray of shrapnel from big, 122 mm Russian-made Katyusha rockets. A fiery fragment could sever an artery. The Marine assignment had become keeping the peace in a madhouse. Peace was being shot away by an ancient Mideast feud between Jews, Muslims, and Christians that confounded Geraghty. Angered by the attack on the visiting brass, Geraghty ordered his 155 mm howitzers and—for the first time—5-inch shells from the

USS *Bowen*, a warship in Beirut harbor. They silenced the offending Shuf Mountain battery.

The men in the meeting were listening to the commander of the Lebanese army, a three-star, about resumption of a century-old Shuf Mountain war. The aide sidled up once more to pull Geraghty aside. He hunched over and whispered in Geraghty's ear.

"Sir, you have to take this call," his aide said.

The Marines were deployed on the worst possible low ground around Beirut International Airport. To keep Israeli forces away from Lebanon's only airport, the US embassy rejected pleas from at least three commanders for a base on higher ground. To the Marines' backs were airport runways and then the shore of the blue Mediterranean. The Marines were sitting ducks for artillery, rocket, mortar, and sniper fire from the looming Shuf Mountains. Their mission was to be a neutral buffer between factions with unsettled ancient vendettas. Geraghty limited his infantry to a self-defense Condition 4: *No bullets in rifle chambers. Withhold fire unless directly threatened.* The Rules of Engagement were becoming meaningless. Peacekeeping had become a bloody joke. Geraghty was restricting use of his artillery and mortars to tit-for-tat: Fire on the Marines and—after a warning—the Marines will shoot back. But he was determined to avoid using offshore fighter-bombers and warship guns that could destroy everything in the mountains above.

The Marines were under attack by different Arab factions. Ragheads, his Marines called them. On that day, Geraghty was being bombarded by Shiite Muslims who wore the lacy, filigreed white skullcaps of the Druse mountain tribe. For 100 years, the Druse exchanged massacres with the Maronite Christians, and the blood feud was under way once more. The Druse leader—the bey—was Walid Jumblatt. In leather jacket, boots, and blue jeans, Jumblatt

prowled the mountain battlefield aboard a Harley-Davidson motor-
cycle. Once inside Christian mountain villages that day, the Druse
favored knives for the slaughter. The Christian leader was Amin Gemayel, who had replaced his assassinated brother, Bashir, as president
of Lebanon. That title and pressure from Israel resulted in US political
and military support for Gemayel's Christians. Confident of support
from American warships in Beirut harbor, Gemayel's Christian militia
had initiated attacks on Jumblatt and his Druse mountain villages
a week earlier. Almost every Shuf village had an outdoor restaurant
where blue smoke from the grill mixed with the perfume of cedars
and eucalyptus. Now, many smelled of cordite and blood.

While Geraghty tried to cling to his role as an even-handed, independent, and neutral peacekeeper, Walid Jumblatt saw the Marines
as part and parcel of the Christian attacks that fell on Druse villages
in the Shuf Moutains that overlooked Beirut. Jumblatt's artillery
and ammunition bombarding the Marines came by mountain road
from Syria and its astute president, Hafez al-Assad. Assad had just
been rearmed by his military patron, the Soviet Union. And the Syrian leader was in league with Iran's Ayatollah Ruhollah Khomeini,
the black-eyed Shia leader of extremist Islam.

Who was the enemy? Iran? The Soviet Union? Syria? Jumblatt?
There was even a splinter of the Palestinian Liberation Organization
taking potshots at the Marines. It was a lethal mix. In addition, nine
other militias in Beirut would throw up roadblocks. Teenagers with
AK-47 machine guns extracted tolls. One militia unit stole all the
Volvos from the Swedish embassy. Another invaded high-rise buildings to pitch their enemies from the rooftops.

Geraghty and his Marines were caught up in Israel's ambition to
wrest Syria's de facto control of Lebanon and humiliate its Soviet

patron. President Ronald Reagan had signed on to Israel's strategy. To him, it was part of his global anti-Soviet crusade that included both Kremlin clients, Syria and the Palestine Liberation Organization. That Israeli-American goal vanished in bomb blasts, the assassination of Bashir Gemayel, and the massacre at the Sabra and Shatila refugee camps that shocked the world.

Geraghty, a Marine infantry officer, knew little of this a few months earlier. His view of the world barely extended beyond the training, care, and feeding of his 2,100 men detached from the 2nd Marine Division at Camp Lejeune. The 1,200 Marine infantry troops under fire were supported by Marine warplanes and helicopters units offshore. Geraghty was struggling to avoid being drawn deeper into this viper's den of Levant bloodletting. It would jeopardize his troops and his role as commander of the Marines and French, British, and Italian troops that made up a multinational peacekeeping force of 5,000. His ground forces were badly outgunned. The Americans' deployment in sandbag-protected foxholes scattered on the hateful low ground made them particularly vulnerable. Statistically, artillery was the biggest killer on the battlefield. An unstoppable direct hit left bloody bits and pieces. Geraghty's determined neutrality for the multinational force was being eroded—blown away—almost daily. The colonel was on the spot.

Once more, the aide pleaded with him to pick up the phone: Silver Screen Six was calling.

"Who is that?" Geraghty demanded. He had never heard of Silver Screen Six.

It was Marine code for Ronald Wilson Reagan, POTUS—president of the United States—and CINC: commander in chief of all US military forces, including Geraghty's bloodied 24th Marine Amphibious Unit. In Washington, the Secret Service code name for

Reagan was Rawhide. The cowboy touch pleased Reagan. In Beirut that day, his Marine code name reflected Hollywood with a military flair. The Six added to Silver Screen was the infantry radio designation for the commander in chief of all Marine forces deployed around the globe. The Six designation originated with the US infantry in World War II. The commander of a regiment was usually a full bird colonel such as Geraghty, a grade OS-6 in US officer rankings. Soon, every commander down to the platoon level was designated as the Six. For example, the commander of Charlie Company would answer "Charlie Six" on the radio net.

The Marines in Beirut were Silver Screen Six's first command of troops under fire. The killing and wounding of Marine infantry was also drawing political blood from the president. What to do? Reagan's military judgment was based heavily on celluloid bravura.

Dogfighting the Nazis with his Royal Air Force Spitfire, well, that was all make-believe in the movie *International Squadron.* Reagan's other warfare experience came from making training films for the War Department during World War II. In 1943 he was sent to the Provisional Task Force Show Unit producing the morale-boosting *This Is the Army,* which won the Academy Award for Best Original Score. It was the closest Reagan came to the Oscar coveted by all Hollywood. But Reagan was a soldier with more time in grade than bogus studio colonels. He had enlisted in the Army in 1937 as a private following completion of 14 home-study courses. His degree from Eureka College elevated him one month later to 2nd lieutenant in the Calvary Reserves in Des Moines, Iowa. One attraction was the uniform. In that day it was the Sam Browne belt over the tunic and the flared breeches—the British jodhpurs—tucked into high leather boots with spurs.

Ordered to active duty in 1942, Reagan was first the liaison officer organizing truck transport for troops to be loaded on ships at the San Francisco Port of Embarkation. Terrible eyesight made him unsuited for overseas deployment. By then, he was a veteran of 30 movies and was soon transferred to the 1st Motion Picture Unit in Culver City. More conventional khaki with captain bars was worn at Hollywood parties during the war years. Roles including a P-40 Warhawk fighter ace turned instructor and a chaplain who would be killed by Japanese artillery were part of distinctive and effective training films. The hitch left him with an abiding admiration for the military and its capabilities. He was the first modern president to return salutes with military vigor: bring the up slow like honey and then bring it down sharp. Saluting Marines at the bottom of his helicopter stairs always got a snappy return. The military bearing was familiar to the nation from footage of his return from Camp David or global trips.

Reagan first dispatched the Marines to Beirut in August 1982. Geraghty was the fourth commander of the rotating Marine units. His Marine Amphibious Unit was a self-contained MAU supported by artillery, helicopters, and warplanes aboard ships in Beirut harbor. None of the offshore warships or Marine rifles were needed for the first 13 months. But in the first week of September 1983, things quickly fell apart. A big reason was Israel's retreat from Beirut despite Reagan's pleas to hold fast at Shuf Mountain checkpoints. In a phone call to Prime Minister Menachem Begin on September 3, Reagan asked for more time. It would give Lebanese army troops—a government force independent of Christian militias—a chance to take over Israeli positions and halt Druse attacks. They were American trained and equipped with US artillery and tanks.

"I'm sure you are aware of the massacre that has taken place there," Reagan told the Israeli prime minister. "The men, women, and children in that Christian village that were massacred. Could you delay a few more days in that withdrawal until the Lebanese army can free itself from Beirut and move into the [Shuf]?"

Begin said Israel had delayed long enough. "I know that the evacuation had to start tonight," he told Reagan. Begin's refusal of Reagan's request was just one more in a series of rejections over the past two years. Begin and his minister of defense, Ariel Sharon, had induced Reagan to support the old but dubious Jerusalem goal: a peace treaty with Beirut Christians that would break Syria's control of Lebanon. For two years, Begin and Sharon had duped, misled, and lied to Reagan. Now, the American president was as blood-stained as the rest of the political players. His personal emissary had secretly promised US protection for undefended Palestinian women and children who were later massacred by Christian militias. Sharon's use of Israeli troops to support the Sabra and Shatila slaughter ignited global outrage and revulsion in the Oval Office. Israeli voters angry over their army's actions in Beirut pressured the Jerusalem government to leave. Now the grand ambition in Lebanon was ending in a bloody fiasco. Reagan and his Marines were left holding the Beirut bag.

Hundreds of Israeli tanks and trucks roared away September 4. Unhindered by the Israel Defense Forces in the Shuf, Christian militia troops from East Beirut quickly attacked their ancient enemy, the Druse. President Gemayel was confident of support from Colonel Geraghty's Marines and naval power just offshore. With weapons supplied by Syria, the Druse fought back and also fired on the American positions below. American support for the Christian Lebanese government made the troops legitimate targets for Walid Jumblatt and Druse artillery.

Silver Screen Six's command was under fire, and political shrapnel had reached the Oval Office. Some Democrats in Congress demanded Reagan invoke the War Powers Act now that the Marines were embattled. That would give Congress a veto over Reagan's decision to put US forces in harm's way. Some Democrats called the deployment a blunder and threatened a withdrawal order, humiliating the Republican president. Only Congress was empowered by the Constitution to declare war. But the president, with command of the military, usurped that authority, as did John F. Kennedy and Lyndon B. Johnson in launching the Vietnam War. Congress was left with Hobson's choice: approve a resolution of support or vote against American boys in combat. It was after the humiliating defeat in Vietnam that Congress had passed the War Powers Act, which dictates that once the act is invoked, US forces must be withdrawn after 60 days unless Congress approves continued operations. The politics of the deployment in Lebanon unnerved White House advisers. American voters would decide Reagan's reelection in the coming year. The New Hampshire primary was six months away. White House polls were a red flag.

"I'm up on job rating . . . ," Reagan noted in his diary. "But on foreign policy—Lebanon I'm way down. The people just don't know why we're there." With the Marine deaths, Reagan began to reinforce American ground forces. He ordered a second Marine amphibious unit of 2,100 to stand offshore in Beirut harbor. The 31st MAU was en route. It signaled American determination to stay and fight. Reagan got a taste of voter sentiment when he called the parents of two Marines killed in Beirut September 7. They were Lance Corporal Randy Clark of Minong, Wisconsin, and Corporal Pedro Valle of San Juan, Puerto Rico. Valle's platoon sergeant stumbled on what he thought was some broken tree limbs but turned out to be Valle, torn apart by a direct hit from a 122 mm Druse rocket. The attack also killed Clark. Reagan knew only that they were dead. "Not easy. One father asked if they were in Lebanon for anything that was worth his son's life," he wrote in his diary. Reagan was on the spot.

What had been a feud between the Defense and State Departments from the outset of his administration now filled the 72-year-old president's brain with conflicting advice, often beyond his comprehension. Defense Secretary Caspar Weinberger, opposed to deploying the Marines in the first place, now wanted them withdrawn. Secretary of State George Shultz, a World War II Marine combat officer, saw no reason to "cut and run." Shultz appealed to Reagan's sense of Marine heroics—stand and fight. "We needed to stand firm, showing strength that was purposeful and steady," Shultz argued. Reagan hated their disunity. As governor of California, he simply ordered the combatants to work out an agreement. And they did. But Washington was not Sacramento. Reagan's thought process might involve Marine Sergeant John M. Stryker— John Wayne—in *Sands of Iwo Jima*. Old movies were always mixed into the president's perception of events. "He frequently conflated old movies with issues that confronted him," said Ken Khachigian, a Reagan speechwriter.

The old Warhawk ace favored a devastating air strike on the Ragheads. "I can't get the idea out of my head," Reagan wrote, "that some F14s off the Eisenhower coming in at about 200 ft. over the Marines & blowing the hell out of a couple of artillery emplacements would be a tonic for the Marines & at the same time would deliver a message to those gun happy middle east terrorists." American voters might get a whiff of victory! The romantic belief that airpower could settle a ground war seduced more than one president during the Vietnam War. Endless Hollywood warplane epics showed an enemy destroyed by aerial bombardment. But after World War II, US surveys showed that Nazi armament production continued despite almost constant aerial bombardment. In fact, the warplanes of today that come and go over the battlefield can pave the way for boots on the ground. As the planes zoom away, they leave the question: What happens next? American bombing of North Vietnam was the prelude to an endless ground war. Dead Americans—58,318 of them—and 153,303 troops hospitalized in Vietnam dominated the thinking of the Joint Chiefs of Staff. Bumbling diplomats could trigger a ground war with fast-fading public support. Army General John Vessey, chairman of the Joint Chiefs, was dead set against aerial bombardment in Beirut.

Reagan's wishful air-strike diary entry was on September 7, the day before Silver Screen Six decided to call Colonel Geraghty. The president's blood was up and an air attack on the Druse was in his thoughts when he made the call.

The three generals glared as the colonel left the crisis meeting to take the call. With his aide still hovering, Geraghty finally picked up the phone and identified himself. A voice said: "Colonel, this is the White House. Stand by for the President." It was 9:53 a.m. in Washington when Reagan connected with Geraghty. The president expressed the entire nation's pride at the outstanding job being done against difficult odds and said he would provide "whatever support it takes to stop the attacks." Geraghty promised that he and his men would "hang tough and carry out the mission." After hearing the president praise the Marine effort, Geraghty told him "we truly appreciated his support and leadership. I ended with 'Semper Fi, Mr. President.'" Geraghty would learn that *Semper Fidelis*—Always Faithful—was a one-way street with Reagan.

There is likely a White House recording of the conversation, but it still has a security classification at the Reagan Presidential Library in Simi Valley, California. There is no mention of the phone call in Reagan's diary; Geraghty's version is sparse and he would not elaborate in an interview with me. "I don't want to get into it," Geraghty said.

Washington's shifting priorities rarely bother frontline officers such as Geraghty. They take orders from the nearest superior and march on. But the commander in chief telephoned the lowly Marine colonel 5,000 miles away for one big reason: Only Geraghty could decide to shift from peacekeeping to warfare in Beirut.

Only he could order the 5-inchers on warships in the harbor or F-14 Tomcat squadrons and all kinds of fighters, bombers, and helicopters from two aircraft carriers. Every rifle shot had to be approved by Geraghty. No general, no admiral, no White House interloper, no American ambassador could overrule Geraghty without violating the sacrosanct chain of command. Geraghty knew his mission was increasingly in conflict with the realities of Beirut. And when he finally picked up the phone, he knew Silver Screen Six was at the top of a twisted chain of command responsible for conflicting orders in Beirut. Hanging tough, Geraghty would soon learn, was becoming impossible.

Reagan's phone call on September 8, 1983, was no pep talk. He was the head hawk. The president's faction of the American government—the National Security Council and Shultz—wanted Geraghty to subdue the Arabs, oust Syria from Lebanon, and even enable a peace treaty between the Jews and the Christians in Lebanon. Reagan was going to succeed where Begin and Sharon had failed. "Doing Israel's dirty work," complained an editorial in *The New York Times*. Secretary of State Shultz wanted to back the plan with US naval gunfire and fighter-bombers from the deck of the USS

Dwight D. Eisenhower. There were 12,000 men offshore aboard six warships in the American carrier battle group. France moved its carrier *Foch* within striking distance. The doves, led by Defense Secretary Weinberger, worried about possible reprisals against the Marines. He reflected the perspective of the military commanders who viewed Geraghty's light infantry as too light. Weinberger wanted Geraghty out of the vulnerable airport deployment and back to their offshore barracks, the Marine assault ship USS *Iwo Jima.*

Shultz and Weinberger were influenced by the April bombing of the American embassy in Beirut six months earlier, but in dramatically different ways. A military strike would redress the outrage against Shultz's diplomats. The embassy's location near the elegant seaside corniche in Beirut symbolized American influence and power. Now the wreckage was proof that the United States was something of a paper tiger. US reprisals—the coin of the Beirut realm—never happened. But for Weinberger, the terrorist's ability to drive his bomb-laden van into the lobby of the embassy underscored the vulnerability of American troops in Beirut. Weinberger was backed by the Joint Chiefs of Staff. The top brass was unified by the lessons of Vietnam. Small clashes could suck the United States into a major land war followed by deaths, loss of domestic political support, retreat, and humiliation. The post–Vietnam Syndrome dominated the Pentagon.

Joining this clash between the biggest bulls in Washington was the national security adviser to the president, William P. Clark. He listened in as Reagan talked to Colonel Geraghty on September 8. For two years, Clark had failed in his crucial job of compromising disputes between State and Defense. He had thrown up his hands at the increasing hostility between Weinberger and Shultz.

On Beirut, Reagan and Clark supported Shultz's game plan. Why finance this massive Pentagon budget if military force couldn't back US diplomacy? Shultz's bellicosity, however, was stifled by the defense secretary. Weinberger controlled Beirut through his chain-of-command control of the Joint Chiefs of Staff, including the Marine Corps commandant—Geraghty's superior. The Chiefs, afflicted with the sour aftertaste of Vietnam, wanted the Marines out of Beirut.

To bypass Weinberger and the top brass—and Geraghty—the White House inserted its own man in Beirut, carrying Reagan's ultimate authority.

The man selected was to be the president's special representative in the Middle East, Ambassador Robert Carl McFarlane.

Somehow, McFarlane, a master of the military and bureaucracy, could weave around Weinberger, the Chiefs, and the bird colonel, Geraghty. McFarlane could deliver on the president's wishes. Reagan envisioned Tomcats from the *Ike* roaring low over embattled Marines and blasting those white skullcaps off the Druse cannoneers. McFarlane had to overcome the secretary of defense, the Joint Chiefs, the post–Vietnam Syndrome, and, perhaps the smallest obstacle, the boyish-looking Marine Colonel Timothy Geraghty. McFarlane had to make it happen.

Bud McFarlane was on the spot.

11

Moment of Truth

Walid Jumblatt's Druse cannoneers dropped a round into the front yard of the residence of the US ambassador to Lebanon. It might have been a stray from a nearby mountain war, or a deliberate message. But the explosion alarmed Robert McFarlane, President Reagan's personal representative to the Mideast, who had directed many a howitzer at the Viet Cong. Then an incoming round sent McFarlane scrambling for shelter. He gathered his staff, who had been imported directly from the White House National Security Council. Together they squeezed into the residence's bomb shelter with complaints that it was no bigger than a closet.

If truth be known, Ambassador Robert Dillon would have liked to lock McFarlane and his staff in that closet. Dillon had begun referring to them as "the President's men" and those "NSC sons-of-bitches." They cut him off from all their activities until McFarlane blundered into a diplomatic minefield. Amin Gemayel, the president of Lebanon, talked McFarlane into cutting off US relations with Jumblatt and his Druse army of 8,000 fighters. "It illustrated the problems of dealing with people who don't understand the situation on the ground," Dillon said. Gemayel was no bipartisan leader of Lebanon but a foppish Christian leader who sparked the mountain war by attacking the Druse once Israeli forces withdrew from the Shuf Mountains. Gemayel was hoping to snare McFarlane and the United States into his crusade against the hated Jumblatt. The Christian-Druse blood feud was at least two centuries old. Now, on impulse, McFarlane threw aside US policy to mediate the dispute with contacts to both leaders. "I immediately protested," Dillon said. "McFarlane was clearly so wrong that six weeks later, McFarlane, without admitting he was wrong, withdrew his objections and in fact personally started dealing with the Druse."

McFarlane had been seduced by the Christians, as were many in Beirut. Some of their parties at exquisite mountainside homes in East Beirut "were better than anything you would see in New York or Paris," Colonel Geraghty recalled. Beautiful women draped in diamonds and the lowest-cut dresses entertained. The finest French champagne was served with caviar and smoked salmon on silver platters. "I could have lived on those platters," Ambassador Dillon said.

Once more angered by McFarlane, Dillon regretted his offer to let him and his staff stay at the ambassador's residence. They hid all their actions from Dillon, the State Department, and the Central Intelligence Agency. Dillon tried to have his deputy, Ryan Crocker, sit in on their meetings. McFarlane refused. "They didn't trust him [Crocker] because he spoke Arabic and was therefore probably pro-Arab. Instead of using those government communication channels, McFarlane set up a satellite phone connected directly to William Clark, the NSC director, at the White House. Clark dealt directly with Reagan. No one on the NSC staff spoke Arabic. None were area experts," Dillon said. In addition, an Army brigadier general,

Carl Stiner, representing the Pentagon's Joint Chiefs, was attached to McFarlane's staff. Stiner set up his phone link to the Pentagon in the building next to Dillon's swimming pool. More secrets from the ambassador on the spot. "It was a text-book version of how not to run things," Dillon said.

McFarlane's real mission began to emerge with his first clashes with Marine Colonel Geraghty. The Marine leader was struggling to keep the multinational force and his troops out of the spreading mountain war between Jumblatt's Druse on one side and the Lebanese Armed Forces (LAF) and Gemayel's Christian militias on the other. Dillon watched as McFarlane pushed the Marines into the fight. "McFarlane and Co. were constantly coming up with schemes that would have required naval gun-fire or [aircraft] forays from ships anchored off the coast," Dillon said, because "they believed they had a duty to somehow restore the use of military force as an American policy option." But, he noted, "the Marine officers were in increasing opposition to Bud McFarlane and his team."

Geraghty was convinced McFarlane was on the road to disaster. "I wondered if anyone else realized where this fucking train was headed," Geraghty grumbled. Only Geraghty had the authority to order American forces to shift from peacekeeping to warmaking. And his opposition was backed up by the secretary of defense and the Joint Chiefs of Staff in Washington.

Tensions rose between the commander of all forces in Beirut and Reagan's man on the scene. On September 10, Jumblatt's forces, using weapons supplied by Syria, launched a major offensive against the LAF and Gemayel's Phalange militia. The Lebanese army was rebuilt by US Army trainers in 1982 and equipped with more than $1 billion worth of weapons, tanks, and artillery. Soldiers from all religious groups—Sunni and Shiite Muslims, Druse, Christian—

were recruited for a newly integrated force. US Special Forces trainers wondered if the new army would disintegrate along factional
lines once the fighting began. So the first test was in a market town,
Suq el Gharb, just north of Beirut, where the Lebanese and Phalange forces set up defensive positions. The village was seven miles
from the suburb of Yarze, the location of the American ambassador's residence, the Ministry of Defense, and the Presidential Palace.

The Lebanese casualty list after the first night of fighting was not
high—seven killed and 48 wounded. But when McFarlane saw the
tally, it convinced him that the Syrian-backed Druse would quickly
overwhelm the Lebanese forces. On September 11, McFarlane dispatched a "flash" cable to NSC chief William Clark at the White House:

"There is a serious threat of a decisive military defeat which
could involve the fall of the GOL [Government of Lebanon] within
twenty-four hours. Last night's battle was waged within five kilometers of the Presidential Palace. . . . This is an action message. A
second attack against the LAF is expected this evening.

"Ammunition and morale are very low and raise serious possi-
bilities that an enemy brigade will break through and penetrate the
Beirut perimeter. In short, tonight we could be in enemy lines."

Dillon was aghast when he saw the message. First, he and his
staff were confident that the Lebanese army troops under Colonel Michel Aoun could withstand Druse attacks. Even if Jumblatt's
forces broke through, they were hardly the "enemy." "We had good
relations with the Druse," Dillon said.

Geraghty, too, doubted McFarlane's assessment. "My multiple
intelligence sources revealed they were holding up well," Geraghty
said of the Lebanese army brigade. "Their defenses were strong and
responsive. They appeared to be fighting together with determination in repulsing several fierce attacks."

McFarlane was on fire. The Druse shell that sent him scrambling with his staff for shelter was a turning point. "It was time for the Marines to fire back," he said. Despite the incoming, he raced 20 yards over open ground to his satellite phone center. He called Clark at the White House. "Our basic strategy is on the line here," McFarlane told Clark. Instead of a battle between Druse and Christian forces, McFarlane portrayed it as an effort by Syrian president Assad to overthrow the government of Lebanon. Anticipating Defense Secretary Weinberger's opposition, McFarlane said the White House must realize the danger. "You do face the undeniable reality that Americans are also under fire and the existing rules of engagement provide authority for returning fire if you're being fired on," McFarlane told Clark.

Exactly what Clark told the president remains unknown. Perhaps he evoked an image of a desperate Colonel Henry Fonda fighting off a swarm of attackers in the 1948 film *Fort Apache*. Reagan tended to conflate old movies with pressing reality, and McFarlane had reported they were under fire. Whatever was said, Silver Screen Six authorized the unleashing of American aircraft and naval gunfire for the Suq el Gharb battle.

When challenged later about his personal input into Marine operations in Beirut at a news conference, Reagan became agitated. "Let me set the record straight on that," Reagan said. "All that I did—I don't give tactical orders to the military when there is a mission that has been approved to be carried out."

But that is exactly what he did on September 11 in a specific and detailed order to Geraghty.

"It has been determined that occupation of the dominant terrain in the vicinity of SUQ-AL-GHARB . . . is vital to the safety of US personnel (USMNF [multinational force], other US military personnel in Beirut, and the U.S. diplomatic presence)," Reagan's order said. "As a consequence, when the US ground commander determines that SUQ-AL-GHARB is in danger of falling as a result of attack involving non-Lebanese forces and if requested by the host government, appropriate US assistance in defense of SUQ-AL-GHARB is authorized. Assistance for this specific objective may include naval gun fire support and, if deemed necessary, tactical air strikes, but shall exclude ground forces." It was signed "Ronald Reagan" and filed as an addendum to National Security Decision Directive 103, "Strategy for Lebanon," issued on September 10.

The Joint Chiefs relayed the order from the Pentagon to Geraghty, telling him the change in the ground rules was made "over the strong objections of Secretary of Defense Weinberger." It, too, spelled out the three conditions for using firepower: Suq el Gharb was in danger of falling, the government of Lebanon requested support, and the attacking force was non-Lebanese. According to Geraghty, the Pentagon version emphasized that "nothing in this message shall be construed as changing the mission for the U.S. Multinational Force."

Geraghty knew it changed everything. "It would mark that the Marines, for the first time, were going on the offensive in direct support of the LAF," Geraghty said. "I understood, all too well, the consequences of this decision. For all practical purposes, it would eliminate whatever appearance of neutrality and impartiality we had left."

Reagan and McFarlane had visions of F-14 Tomcat fighter-bombers from the USS *Eisenhower* streaking over Suq el Gharb with napalm and white phosphorous to obliterate the Soviet-backed troops and armor. But Geraghty made sure it never happened. "What followed was a rancorous week of requests by McFarlane and members of his staff to allow the use of naval gunfire and air strikes," Geraghty said. "To their great consternation, I blocked these requests."

Eyewitnesses recounted to me how McFarlane accused Geraghty of "ignoring a direct order from the president of the United States." Stiner, the Army brigadier general on McFarlane's staff, also pressured Geraghty. But the Marine colonel would not budge.

Geraghty recalled a screaming match with Stiner. "I yelled, 'General, don't you realize we'll pay the price down here? We'll get slaughtered! We're totally vulnerable!'" In a confrontation with McFarlane, Geraghty refused demands for naval gunfire and tactical aircraft. "Sir, I can't do that. This will cost us our neutrality. Don't you realize we'll get slaughtered down here? We're sitting ducks!"

At one point, Stiner got Pentagon approval for an air strike on a specific target he submitted to the Joint Chiefs as a map with a target grid. But Geraghty defied him. "I refused the air strike mission," he said.

Geraghty was emboldened, as it appeared that McFarlane was something of a Chicken Little with predictions of the sky falling. Instead of collapsing on September 11, the 8th Brigade of the Lebanese army, resupplied by US Marines, was fending off Jumblatt's attacks. But by September 16, Geraghty detected increased support by Syria and Iranians from Baalbek. Heavy artillery fell on the US ambassador's residence and the nearby Ministry of Defense. "The stakes continued to be raised," Geraghty said. He authorized the USS *Bowen* and the USS *John Rodgers* in Beirut harbor to fire 72 rounds on six separate targets. But Geraghty rejected air strikes, a setback for Reagan's vision of carrier warplanes zooming over the Druse gun batteries.

By September 19, Geraghty's radio intercepts showed a dramatic increase in Syrian and Iranian forces supporting Jumblatt's Druse. A massive attack was forming, including Russian-made tanks. The Lebanese army formally requested Geraghty's support. Fear of a Lebanese army collapse, foreign troops involved in the attack, and

a request for help from the government of Lebanon—all three re-
quirements listed in Reagan's order. Geraghty moved four warships
closer to shore. Aircraft from the *Eisenhower* and the French aircraft carrier *Foch* were sent aloft to guide naval gunfire. "There was
no reason to order any air strikes," Geraghty said.

The *Bowen* and the *Rodgers,* along with the USS *Virginia* and
the USS *Radford,* aimed 360 rounds of high explosives at the Druse,
Syrians, and Iranians at Suq el Gharb. The assault was disrupted,
and the attackers retreated. Geraghty had doubts that the US naval
gunfire was actually necessary. In his opinion, the Lebanese army had
only light casualties—eight killed and 12 wounded. The Lebanese
performed beyond his expectations.

McFarlane was pleased with that, but upset with American journalists reporting that Gemayel's Phalange militia also took part in
the fight against the Druse. He singled out *The New York Times* for
reporting that the United States was taking the side of the Maronite
Christians in the ancient feud. "Nevertheless, the situation after the
battle was promising," McFarlane concluded. A cease-fire between
Christians and Druses was negotiated by Saudi Arabia. McFarlane
headed back to Washington, DC, where he soon replaced Clark as
Reagan's adviser on national security affairs. From the role of a
slavish Marine major, McFarlane had ascended to Henry Kissinger's
post. McFarlane had big plans.

Back in Beirut, Geraghty had growing doubts that the American
firepower was really needed on September 19. "It was another occasion when I wondered if we had been had," Geraghty said. He told
his staff about his misgivings.

His gut instinct was that the Corps would pay in blood.

12

Burying the Marines

Colonel Timothy Geraghty, still ankle-deep in his slaughtered Beirut command, was surprised at the arrival of the president. François Mitterrand had come with France's condolences. At almost the same moment 241 Americans were killed on that Sunday morning of October 23, 1983, another truck bomb struck the French headquarters. It killed 58 French soldiers and wounded scores. First thing Monday, Mitterrand flew to Beirut. These were his troops. He had sent them into harm's way. They were part of an American-commanded multinational force, and he had supported its mission. Once he had tended to the French troops, Mitterrand rode to the nearby American compound. A 40-foot concrete and steel barracks was now a hole full of broken slabs crushing moaning Marines. Smells of feces, blood, and sun-ripened flesh hung in the air. Pieces of Marines were still being recovered. A Marine in a sleeping bag was impaled on a tree limb. Such a walkthrough would be enough for any other visiting head of state. Not Mitterrand. He proceeded to a nearby Lebanese air force hangar that had become a makeshift morgue for Geraghty's dead.

It was dark inside, where almost 200 bodies in green body bags had been placed in aluminum containers called transfer cases. Many of the body bags contained only body parts. The transfer cases were stacked four wide and four high on aluminum pallets. There were 16 transfer cases on each pallet, secured by nylon straps. The rows of pallets seemed endless. It took a moment for Mitterrand's eyes to adjust to the darkness. He was astonished.

"His eyes opened wide and his face became pallid," Geraghty said. "It was an expression that I will take to my grave."

In a classic Gallic gesture, Mitterrand raised both arms with palms skyward. He implored heaven for an answer to the enormity of so many young men in tragic death. Before each stacked pallet, Mitterrand made the sign of the cross and said a silent prayer. When he was done, Mitterrand asked to inspect a floodlit area blocked by curtains in the back of the hangar. Inside, bits and pieces of Marines were being assembled in body bags. "Again, Mitterrand and his party paid their solemn respects to the fallen peacekeepers," Geraghty said. "It convinced me that the French will stand with us in times of bad fortune." Six more Marines had yet to die. They were being crushed between concrete slabs too big to be removed in time. Navy corpsmen injected morphine as they slipped away.

There were no personal condolences from Silver Screen Six, no phone call like the one Geraghty received a month earlier promising the president's full support. Reagan was probably wrestling with his conscience: Should he have listened to his secretary of defense a week earlier? After US naval gunfire on Muslim forces in September, there was an upsurge in attacks and threats against the Marines in October. While many threats were unspecific, at least some pointed to the Marine barracks. "We had good intelligence before the attack," a senior Army officer told me a week after the attack. But the threats became too much for Defense Secretary Caspar Weinberger. He arranged a crucial meeting with Reagan on the Beirut deployment. Weinberger and the Joint Chiefs of Staff wanted the Marines removed to the safety of their ships offshore. It was eight days before a suicide driver guided a yellow Mercedes stake truck inside the barracks where 350 Marines were sleeping.

"I begged the President at least to pull them back and put them back on their transports as a more defensible position," Weinberger recounted in a 2002 interview. He told Reagan: "[They're] sitting in a bull's-eye. . . . They're in a position of extraordinary danger. They have no mission. They have no capability of carrying out a mission, and they're terribly vulnerable." But National Security Adviser Robert McFarlane and Secretary of State George Shultz stood firm. . . . "When that horrible tragedy came, . . . I took it very personally and still feel responsible in not having been persuasive enough to overcome the arguments that the 'Marines don't cut and run,' and, 'We can't leave because we're there,' and all of that."

Geraghty and his dead were getting an American presidential cold shoulder. Reagan made only a brief statement on return from a golfing weekend at Augusta National. "I know there are no words that can express our sorrow and grief over the loss of those splendid young men and the injury to so many others," Reagan said.

Reagan did send Vice President George H. W. Bush. In helmet and flak jacket, Bush visited for an hour but said little. Geraghty got a better idea of Washington's reaction with the arrival of a congressional delegation on a firsthand inspection three days after the bombing. Kentucky Republican Larry J. Hopkins raced up and placed his face within an inch of Geraghty's nose.

"You are going to eat a shit sandwich," Hopkins yelled.

Crude as Hopkins was, it was an accurate prediction. Geraghty was quickly relieved of command. Reagan ordered a Pentagon investigation that wound up making the sandwich that ended the Marine commander's career. Geraghty's failure to guard his Marines on October 23 seemed so complete. In another time of drumhead justice, Hopkins might have arranged a firing squad. A Department of Defense Commission headed by retired admiral Robert Long put together the case against Geraghty. There was no mention of orders from Silver Screen Six.

On orders from Tehran, Iranian Revolutionary Guards and Hezbollah Shiite militia from Baalbek chose Sunday morning, just as Japan did in striking Pearl Harbor in 1944. As they had then, American defenders showed surprise and puzzlement. In Tehran, Iranian Major General Qasem Soleimani, commander of the Revolutionary Guards, had dispatched the explosives to Damascus. They were then shuttled 35 miles to Baalbek and loaded onto the yellow Mercedes stake-bed truck provided by the engineering student Imad Mughniyeh. A suicide driver with black, bushy hair, a moustache, and an open blue-green shirt gunned the diesel vehicle through chest-high rolls of concertina barbed wire. That was the only outer defensive perimeter. Carrying 2,000 pounds of high explosive laced with bottles of butane gas, the truck sped between Guard Posts 6 and 7—manned by Marines ordered to keep their M-16s unloaded. Lance Corporal Henry Linkkila in Post 6 and Lance Corporal Eddie DiFranco in Post 7 knew breaching the wire meant an attack. Gunfire was justified under the Rules of Engagement. Both were marksmen who could have killed the driver with their M-16 rifles, which could fire 13 rounds per second. They had enough ammunition to disable the truck as well. But they were hamstrung by their commander's misgivings. Geraghty, worried about accidental shootings, modified the Rules of Engagement, which called for rifles to be loaded with magazines but have no bullets in the chamber. Linkkila and DiFranco were forbidden to have magazines in their rifles because of Geraghty's concerns. They saw the yellow Mercedes truck in plenty of time. But the extra seconds it took to pull 30-round magazines from waist-belt pouches and slap them in their rifles meant the truck was out of range and untouched. It had already raced through a chain-link gate left open to ease Marine vehicle traffic and was entering the barracks. Sergeant Steven Russell, the sergeant of the guard, was in Guard Post 8, a shack inside the entrance of the Battalion Landing Team barracks where 350 Marines were sleeping in on Sunday morning. Russell watched the roaring diesel truck navigate past a sandbag barrier, then find a narrow opening to steps leading up to the entrance and Guard Post 8. The driver smiled at Russell as the truck climbed the stairs and entered the barracks. "Hit the deck," Russell yelled. There was an orange flash. Steel-reinforced concrete columns 15 feet wide were lifted off their foundations. The building collapsed like a deck of cards.

Silver Screen Six was too busy for anything approaching the French president's expression of grief to the shattered Marines. That Sunday night, Reagan was planning a military operation that might somehow overshadow the devastating video and still photographs coming out of Geraghty's smoking compound. Operation Urgent Fury was designed to shift the world's view from disaster in Beirut to a US invasion of Grenada, a dot in the Caribbean about twice the size of the District of Columbia. But Reagan's plan ran into a formidable roadblock: British prime minister Margaret Thatcher. Grenada was a British crown colony, and to her it was outrageous for the United States to interfere with the local government—no matter how Marxist. Reagan had to excuse himself from a crucial meeting to take her phone call. Howard Baker, his chief of staff, recounted the exchange:

"He went next door from the oval sitting room and closed the door, but as is typical of many people who don't hear very well, he also spoke in a loud voice. I could hear him plain as day. He said, 'Margaret,' long pause. 'But Margaret,' and he went through that about three times and he came back sort of sheepish and said, 'Mrs. Thatcher has strong reservations about this.'"

At the time, Thatcher was in no position for public criticism of Reagan. He had enabled her stunning 1982 victory over Argentina in the Falklands War with US supplies and communications from American bases in the South Atlantic. But in 1984, Thatcher's minister for foreign affairs, Sir Geoffrey Howe, shed some insight on the prime minister's view of the Reagan invasion of Grenada.

"The invasion of Grenada was clearly designed to divert attention," Howe told me in an interview. "You had disaster in Beirut. Now triumph in Grenada. Don't look there. Look over here," he said, gesturing with his forefinger. To Thatcher, who had better information from Grenada, there was no threat to American students, Howe said.

Speaker Tip O'Neill agreed: "Despite what the administration claimed, the students were never in danger, . . . and neither were any of the American residents on the island. But over a hundred American troops were killed or wounded in that operation. We were supposed to be out within 48 hours, but our combat troops stayed on for weeks. And as far as I can see, it was all because the White House wanted the country to forget about the tragedy in Beirut."

Grenada would also enable Reagan's all-important speech to the

nation that would meld victory and tragedy—and let him talk his
way out of trouble. Reagan's emphasis could be heard at the start
of Urgent Fury during a brief White House meeting with reporters
on October 25.

Q: What reports have you received of the success of the operation?

Reagan: Of the initial operation, of landings, securing the immediate targets, taking control of the airports: completely successful! . . .

Q: What's the situation in Lebanon now?

[Deputy Press Secretary Larry Speakes]: I'm sorry, that is the
last question.

Beirut had become the worst moment of his presidency, and his
1984 reelection campaign was off to a bad start. New Hampshire
was only five months away. Operation Urgent Fury would distract
critical questions about Reagan's personal contributions to events
leading up to the Marine massacre. He was haunted by his refusal
to withdraw the Marines to shipboard safety eight days before the
attack. Reagan secretly overruled his top military advisers—Defense
Secretary Weinberger and the Joint Chiefs of Staff—when he ordered Geraghty to use massive naval gunfire in the ancient blood
feud of Muslims versus Christians, abandoning any pretense of being neutral peacekeepers. The September 19 bombardment aligned
the United States on the Christian side. Reagan was still seeking to
drive Syrian troops out of Lebanon as part of a 1982 policy deal
with Israel, but Israel had pulled its troops out of Beirut two weeks
earlier, leaving Reagan to deal with a renewed mountain war. And
the US Navy bombardment of Druse and Syrian forces at Suq el

Gharb had a ripple effect throughout the region. In Damascus, Syrian president Assad realized his support of Walid Jumblatt's Druse army could not defeat a Lebanese government backed by US guns and aircraft just offshore from Beirut. Reagan added to the muscle by ordering the World War II battleship USS *New Jersey* into the Beirut mix on September 26. Its 16-inch guns might reach targets in Damascus, a hint implied by Robert McFarlane during his last meeting with Assad.

The ayatollahs of Tehran may have reached the same decision as Assad. On the very same day the old battleship hove into view, the US National Security Agency intercepted an order from Tehran intelligence to Iran's ambassador to Damascus. It ordered him "to take spectacular action against the American Marines." Four weeks later, the Tehran order led to the yellow Mercedes truck with its smiling suicide driver. Geraghty would not see the intercept until two days after the attack. Belatedly, US intelligence learned that everyone in the Iranian embassy in Damascus fled the facility October 22, the night before the bombing.

Robert Dillon, the American ambassador to Lebanon, saw one miscalculation after another by Reagan and his national security adviser, Robert McFarlane. "It was amateur night," Dillon told me in an interview.

The early October attacks showed ineffective protection for Marines. Poorly rigged dugouts simply would not stop incoming fire. Weinberger, opposed to any hint of a permanent deployment, blocked Navy construction battalions from building rugged defensive positions for Geraghty's troops. Increasingly, Geraghty ordered his infantry out of their exposed foxholes at night to sleep in the safety of the concrete Battalion Landing Team barracks. With the increasing attacks in October, Reagan came under fire in Washington. Four days before the Marine massacre, Reagan was grilled about better protection for the Marines.

> Q: Mr. President, when I was in the marines the doctrine was to take the high ground and hold it and not deploy on a flat, open field like the Beirut airport. What reason is there to prevent the marines from taking some more defensible positions in pursuit of the policy for which you've sent them there?
>
> The President: Well, Jerry [Jeremiah O'Leary, *Washington Times*], all of those things we're asking ourselves, and we're looking at everything that can be done to try and make their position safer. But you must remember, you were talking about when you were being trained as marines for combat. And if these marines had gone there to join in the combat on the side of whatever force we might have picked, then all of those rules would apply. But they're there as part of a multinational force to try and maintain a stability. And their sector happens to be trying to maintain that airport and open it up for traffic. So, airports just happen to be flat. And we're doing everything we can and making everything possible for them to defend themselves.

Reagan's answer reflected his bizarre policy in Beirut—the Marines were under fire but still had to act as neutral peacekeepers, except when they used naval gunfire to bombard the Muslims. The conflict between Washington policy and the reality of Beirut struck Geraghty as he stood in the midst of his dead Marines.

"As I surveyed the carnage, I grew livid," Geraghty said. "I couldn't help thinking: Here lie the fucking unintended consequences of getting sucked into an eight-sided civil war while trying to carry out a peacekeeping mission."

Weinberger, who consistently opposed Reagan's combat plans for US forces in Beirut, became one of the roadblocks to Reagan's invasion of Grenada. The defense chief wanted to delay things for more study. "That meant do nothing," complained Secretary of State George Shultz. Instability surrounding a new leftist government there had worried Reagan for months. He saw a "Cuban-Soviet" ambition to seize the jungle-choked spice island. Proof was a 9,000-foot runway being built by Cuban construction workers. Many islanders saw the project as lifeblood for the tourist industry, replacing a dangerous runway too short for bigger jets.

Perhaps the 581 American students at St. George's University could leave without a fuss on chartered jets or a cruise ship. According to Shultz, both proposals were rejected by Grenada's Revolutionary Military Council. Still, Dr. Geoffrey Bourne, head of the university, said the students were never threatened. Pledges of protection came from the Marxist government, along with food and water for the students—if needed. One US admiral proposed docking in St. George with a landing ship with a Marine contingent as a show of force to evacuate the students. By Saturday night, October 22, political leaders from nearby islands appealed for a US military intervention to crush the left-wing government. Any thought of a two-ship American operation vanished the next day after Reagan learned of the Marine massacre. Skimpy intelligence predicted little opposition: 600 Cuban construction workers who had military training in Cuba and a handful of soldiers under the command of the revolutionary government.

But Reagan girded for something approaching a confrontation with Soviet legions in the Fulda Gap.

On Sunday night, October 23, in the White House Situation Room, National Security Adviser Robert McFarlane was pushing for a much more dramatic invasion. It would include detouring Marines intended to reinforce Geraghty's battered command to Grenada. That set off a nasty confrontation between McFarlane and General Vessey, chairman of the Joint Chiefs. Vessey refused to redirect the Beirut relief force without a direct order from Reagan. McFarlane promptly got the presidential order, and the 22nd Marine Amphibious Unit headed for Grenada, Reagan's new priority. As the night wore on, Reagan assembled a force of at least 14,000. Included were 7,500 sailors and pilots in the USS *Independence* Carrier Strike Force. Ground troops included the 2nd Brigade of the 82nd Airborne Division, Ranger battalions from both the East and West Coasts, two battalions of the 32nd Infantry, the 2nd Battalion of the 8th Marines, and the 160th Aviation Battalion. In addition, Navy SEAL teams, Air Force Combat Control Teams, and Army Special Forces also joined the armada.

Missing was the band of reporters and photographers that accompanied the US military in all its wars. Reagan had ordered Urgent Fury sealed off from the press. Media people aboard a private fleet trying to land on Grenada were threatened with US Navy gunfire. Reporters who made it onto the island were arrested and imprisoned offshore on Navy ships. There would only be one version of events during the two-day conflict—the Reagan administration's. "Completely successful," as Reagan said of the October 25 invasion.

His orders enabled the Pentagon to cover up a series of mishaps that were predictable for such a large force ordered to attack without time to prepare. Most were without a basic map of Grenada. One helicopter crashed after its pilot was shot dead; the Delta Force commandos it was carrying were badly wounded. Four Navy SEALs drowned after jumping from an airplane into seas higher than forecast. Jets from the *Independence* mistakenly bombed a hospital and killed 18 mental patients on October 26. Three Rangers were killed and five others seriously wounded when three helicopters collided on one mission. Most of the 600 Cuban workers surrendered the same day. The Americans killed 25 Cubans and 45 Grenadians. The US toll: 19 killed and 116 wounded. The Marxist leaders vanished.

US military planes began airlifting students on October 27. The students ran off the US Air Force C-141 at Shaw Air Force Base in Columbia, South Carolina. Many fell to their knees and kissed the ground. The joy was an ideal visual setup for Reagan's speech to the nation that night. He had a voice that could transfix listeners as few other presidents. Long after movie directors no longer wanted his face, Hollywood would continue to use his voice in all sorts of films.

Reagan recounted the truck bomb racing past guards in Beirut to stage an attack that would lead to calls for a withdrawal of the Marines. They would stay, the president said.

To Reagan, Soviet ambitions in the Mideast and Latin America were the real cause of turmoil in Beirut and Grenada. "The events in Lebanon and Grenada, though oceans apart, are closely related. Not only has Moscow assisted and encouraged the violence in both countries, but it provided direct support through a network of surrogates and terrorists. . . .

"Grenada, we were told, was a friendly island paradise for tourism. Well, it wasn't. It was a Soviet-Cuban colony, being readied as a major military bastion to export terror and undermine democracy. We got there just in time."

Reagan had a teary finish that recalled his role as George Gipp, near death, telling Notre Dame coach Knute Rockne to remember him to his fellow players someday during a tough football game.

"Ask them to go in there with all they've got and win just one for the Gipper," he said.

Reagan recounted how Marine Corps Commandant General Paul Kelley visited critically injured Marines in an Air Force hospital, quoting him about one "young marine with more tubes going in and out of his body than I have ever seen in one body. He couldn't see very well. He reached up and grabbed my four stars, just to make sure I was who I said I was. He held my hand with a firm grip. He was making signals, and we realized he wanted to tell me something. We put a pad of paper in his hand—and he wrote 'Semper Fi.'"

Reagan resumed in his own words. "Well, if you've been a marine or if, like myself, you're an admirer of the marines, you know those words are a battle cry, a greeting, and a legend in the Marine Corps. They're marine shorthand for the motto of the Corps—'Semper Fidelis'—'always faithful.'"

For Reagan, the speech was a home run.

"The speech must have hit a few nerves . . . ," he wrote that night in his diary. "ABC polled 250 people before the speech, the majority were against us. They polled the same people right after the speech & there had been a complete turn around. 1000's of phone calls & wires from all over the country flooded us more than on any speech or issue since we've been here—10 to 1 in our favor."

Reminders of Beirut kept coming, this time from the military mortuary at Dover Air Force Base in Delaware. National networks broadcast the arrival of the Marines, soldiers, and sailors in aluminum transfer cases on October 27. To arrange ceremonies for 241, planes kept arriving for nine days. Families took charge of the bodies. Silver Screen Six stayed away. Former president Jimmy Carter had showed up at Dover Air Force Base to witness the arrival of

the dead from his ill-fated Desert 1. They were killed as helicopters and rescue planes collided, aborting a planned rescue of US
hostages in Tehran in 1980. But the endless arrival of aluminum
transfer cases was too much for Reagan. On November 4, Reagan
finally delivered his condolences to the Marines of Beirut and their
families at Cherry Point Naval Air Station, adjoining Camp Lejune,
North Carolina.

"I came here today to honor so many who did their duty and
gave that last, full measure of their devotion," Reagan said to a
weeping audience. "They kept faith with us and our way of life. We
wouldn't be free long, but for the dedication of such individuals.
They were heroes. We're grateful to have had them with us."

In political terms, that televised speech to the nation, and his
stage-managing in the Caribbean, put behind Reagan the largest
one-day loss of Marines since Iwo Jima during World War II. When
the Pentagon's Long Commission reported in two months later,
there was no mention of his administration's complicity in events
that led up to the attack. The panel focused on Geraghty and his
guards with unloaded weapons.

Reagan embraced the Long Commission report at a news conference on December 27—two months after the Marine massacre.
But he rejected the panel's call for general courts-martial or other
punishments that could lead to prison and fines.

"I do not believe . . . that the local commanders on the ground,
men who have already suffered quite enough, should be punished
for not fully comprehending the nature of today's terrorist threat.
If there is to be blame, it properly rests here in this Office and with
this President. And I accept responsibility for the bad as well as the
good."

It was another empty gesture that sounded good. A general

court-martial for Geraghty and his deputy, Lieutenant Colonel Howard Gerlach, would have produced defense testimony about the complicity of Reagan, McFarlane, and Schultz. Also untrue was Reagan's claim that Geraghty and Gerlach, now a quadraplegic from the bomb blast, had "suffered quite enough." As commander in chief, he could have blocked—but did not—letters from the secretary of the Navy that ended their careers as Marine officers.

Geraghty's came on February 8, 1984. It ended, "Although this letter will not be placed in your official record, it is intended as a nonpunitive reminder that your actions, as commander, were not sufficient to prevent this tragedy." A terse "John Lehman" was all that followed on the page.

President Anwar Sadat and President Jimmy Carter at the Cairo Airport in 1979. *Courtesy of Bill Foley*

Egyptian president Anwar Sadat in 1980. *Courtesy of Bill Foley*

Patrick J. Sloyan and Ronald Reagan shake hands. *Courtesy of Patrick J. Sloyan*

Reagan cracking jokes. Also pictured, former presidents Gerald Ford, Jimmy Carter, Richard Nixon, former First Lady Rosalyn Carter, and then Vice President George H. W. Bush. *Courtesy of the Ronald Reagan Library*

Reagan chatting with advisors on October 22, 1983, at the Augusta National Golf Club. *Courtesy of the Ronald Reagan Library*

Israeli prime minister Menachem Begin, Egyptian president Anwar Sadat, and Egyptian vice president Hosni Mubarak during a press conference in Cairo in 1979. *Courtesy of Bill Foley*

A smiling Egyptian president Anwar Sadat, moments before he was assassinated on October 6, 1981, known as "The Last Smile." *Courtesy of Bill Foley*

President Reagan in the Oval Office with Israeli prime minister Menachem Begin during a working visit, June 21, 1982. *Courtesy Ronald Reagan Library*

US soldiers running on foot in Beirut. *Courtesy of Bill Foley*

On watch at sea.
*Courtesy of Bill
Foley*

Soldiers on watch. *Courtesy of Bill Foley*

Beirut Shiite demonstration after the marines leave. *Courtesy of Bill Foley*

Beirut marines watch Lebanese student. *Courtesy of Bill Foley*

Shiite women demonstrate in Beirut. *Courtesy of Bill Foley*

On ground in Beirut. *Courtesy of Bill Foley*

A US soldier in Beirut. *Courtesy of Bill Foley*

British soldiers participate in a rescue mission close to the Beirut airport in Lebanon on October 23, 1983. *Courtesy of Bill Foley*

The Reagans mourn after the Beirut US embassy bombing of 1983. *Courtesy of the Ronald Reagan Library*

Palestinian women looking at corpses as they search for missing relatives in the aftermath of the Sabra and Shatila Massacre in Beirut in September 1982. *Courtesy of Bill Foley*

Former US Secretary of State, Henry Kissinger, receiving a kiss from Egyptian president Anwar Sadat's grandson, Sherif, as Sadat and his daughter Jihan look on in Alexandria, Egypt, 1980. *Courtesy of Bill Foley*

13

Path to Iran

A cloud of anguish descended on 241 homes across the United States on Sunday morning October 23, 1983. In Alexandria, Virginia, Deborah Peterson was awakened by her hysterical father, telling her, "Debbie, our worst nightmare has been realized." She turned on the television and saw the smoking ruins of the Marine barracks in Beirut. Her brother, Lance Corporal James Knipple, was there somewhere.

Word of his fate seemed delayed forever. "We watched the television, we got every newspaper, photograph, magazine we could. We looked for his face among the survivors. We even thought we saw him a couple of times." Two weeks later there was a phone call. "They wanted dental information and identifying marks and my father told them about a scar on his forearm," Peterson said. "The next day they told us that he was identified."

A Marine casualty officer came to the house. It was official. Jim was dead. The officer sat next to her father. Both were quiet while the weeping and moaning of family and friends filled the room.

When the house emptied, her father went downstairs. "He started to scream Jim's name over and over and over again at the top of his lungs," Peterson said. "We brought him home on the ninth, on his twenty-first birthday, and we buried him on the tenth, the Marine Corps birthday."

Eighteen years later, Deborah Peterson recounted her grief in the US District Court in Washington, DC. She had instituted a civil action against the Islamic Republic of Iran. After a two-day bench trial in 2003, Judge Royce Lamberth found the Tehran government guilty of the October 24, 1983, Marine attack. Lamberth imposed a $2 billion penalty, a fine simply brushed off by the Iranian government. But almost 1,000 family members affected by the decision persuaded Congress to pass legislation allowing them to seize frozen assets in Bank Markazi (Iran's central bank) in New York. The Supreme Court in 2016 upheld Lamberth's $2 billion penalty in a 6–2 vote. Still, no one has collected a nickel.

Ronald Reagan had vanished into a fog of Alzheimer's by the time of Lamberth's verdict in 2001, yet his presidency was under the microscope throughout the proceedings. Witnesses offered a glimpse into the shadowy war between the United States and Iran that never ends. At the trial, if the evidence presented that Iran staged the attack on the Marines was so certain, why didn't Reagan use unstoppable military power to punish the reckless ayatollahs of Tehran?

Sworn testimony from retired Central Intelligence Agency officers and experts on Iran convinced Lamberth that the president of Iran authorized the bombing of the Marine barracks in 1983. Reagan had vowed to use American power to punish the perpetrators. "We have strong circumstantial evidence that the attack on the Marines was directed by terrorists who used the same method to destroy our embassy in Beirut," Reagan said in a broadcast to the nation. "Those who directed this atrocity must be dealt justice, and they will be."

They never were. Reagan's inaction grated on his generals, American diplomats, and those who paid the price in Beirut. One was retired Lieutenant Colonel Howard Gerlach, Geraghty's deputy. The bomb broke his neck and left the hulking Marine a paraplegic. In sworn testimony from his motorized wheelchair, Gerlach touched on the results that flow from a feckless United States.

"I guess there's three words," said Gerlach in the organized way of Marine officers. "Accountability, deterrence and justice. And they are interrelated. The accountability, and I swear it was on Sunday, I was listening to a rerun of one of the TV—I don't know, Meet the Press or whatever, but Vice President [Dick] Cheney was talking and he was saying that they, the terrorists, feel they can do things with impunity, and he said ever since the Marines in '83. Yes, there hasn't been any accountability."

Declassified records at the Presidential Library in Simi Valley, California, show Reagan was ready to exert some accountability the day after the Marine barracks were destroyed in 1983. There was an edge to Reagan's words during the trans-Atlantic telephone call to President François Mitterrand of France. The American president wanted France to join in a combined attack on those who killed 241 Americans and 58 French soldiers the day before in Beirut. "We're not going to let this terrorist act drive us out of Lebanon and I hope you share that feeling," Reagan said. Mitterrand agreed. Within 24 hours, American intelligence had pinpointed the killers. "We have a great deal of circumstantial evidence that does suggest that the act was actually performed by a group of Iranian radicals, the same ones that destroyed our embassy last April," Reagan said. In a phone call the same day to Prime Minister Thatcher, Reagan was more blunt. "Margaret, the Iranians did it and they are the same ones who blew up our embassy," Reagan said.

Reagan's certainty enabled what the Navy called "a 24-karat gold document" that traced the Iranian suicide driver's orders back to Tehran, which meant to Supreme Leader Ayatollah Ruhollah Khomeini and Ali Akbar Hashemi Rafsanjani, speaker of the Iranian parliament and the second-most powerful person in the government. A month earlier, the US National Security Agency had intercepted a message from Tehran to Damascus. It was from the Ministry of Information Services, which had replaced the secret police force of the deposed shah of Iran. The ministry needed approval from Iran's Supreme National Security Council to send the message, a council controlled by Khomeini and Rafsanjani. In Judge Lamberth's court, Dr. Patrick Clawson, an academic who routinely advised the federal government about Iran, spelled out the link between Tehran and the Marine massacre.

The evidence produced an inescapable conclusion for Judge Lamberth. "The approval of both the Ayatollah Khomeini and President [as of 1989] Rafsanjani was absolutely necessary to carry out the continuing economic commitment of Iran to Hezbollah and to execute the October attack," Lamberth said. "Given their positions of authority, any act of these two officials must be deemed an act of the government of Iran."

Tehran's order was delivered to Iran's ambassador to Syria, Ali Akbar Mohtashemi-Pur. The message from the Tehran leadership directed Mohtashemi-Pur to contact an agent "to take a spectacular action against the United States Marines." The Iranian Revolutionary Guards in Baalbek got the message. And Imad Mughniyeh, the Lebanese engineering student who was enraged by the siege of Beirut, arranged the delivery of the largest nonnuclear bomb in world history. Admiral James Lyons carried the intercept to the secretary of the Navy and the chief of naval operations—two days after the Marine massacre. National Security Agency satellites and computers compiled so much information that it routinely overwhelmed analysts sorting the wheat from the chaff. Although too late to warn Geraghty's Marines, the intercept served as a direct link to the Iranian leadership. More evidence came from remnants of explosives used to destroy both the US embassy and the Marine barracks. It was identified as a non-Western pentaerythritol tetranitrate (PETN), a bulk explosive known to be produced in Iran. And the PETN could not have been shipped to Syria without the approval of the Iranian leadership.

The Joint Chiefs drew up a contingency plan for bombing the Revolutionary Guards headquarters in Tehran. There were plenty of potential military targets, including the massive refinery complex at Abadan, just a few miles inland from the Persian Gulf. There was the network of oil pipelines that shipped 69 percent of the oil that accounted for more than 80 percent of government income. Few Iranians would be killed by blasting the oil facilities, which could be rebuilt. More valuable would be the economic disruption. It could even trigger a revolution that would oust the ayatollahs who had insanely chosen war with the United States. After the Marine massacre, there would be worldwide support for US reprisals. Iran was already seen as a source of terrorism throughout the world.

Of course, such an attack would disrupt the world supply of oil just as prices had begun to stabilize, even decline. Reagan was boasting about the drop at the pump. "You don't have to go any further than the nearest filling station to see that prices have gone down, not up, since decontrol, just as we promised they would," Reagan said in a broadcast to the nation on February 26, 1983.

Soaring prices for Arab oil that had fueled runaway inflation in the United States, along with double-digit interest rates, had ruined Presidents Ford's and Carter's reelection bids. A wrecked US economy and Iran's defiant capture of US embassy staff in Tehran had helped pave the way for Reagan's election. By 1983, Iran had become the second-largest producer and exporter among the Organization of the Petroleum Exporting Countries (OPEC). Nowhere in the files of Reagan's Presidential Library is a document showing any concern about Iran's oil and a reprisal by the United States. Crucial cables and White House documents dealing with that period are still classified secret by the government. Even so, the political explosiveness of Iran's impact on oil prices was almost certain to be considered. Oil figured in almost every Mideast thought and political decision. Suddenly soaring energy prices would have a big impact on Reagan's reelection campaign, which would start in five months. He was off to a bad start with the loss of 241 Americans in the Beirut barracks.

US reprisal contingencies quickly shrank to targets in Lebanon, an ineffective wrist slap. Pinpointed were the quarters for the Iranian Revolutionary Guards in Baalbek, specifically the four-star Al Shams Hotel and the Sheikh Abdullah Barracks. A joint strike was planned to be launched from US and French carriers offshore from Beirut. French and American planners fretted over the ancient Roman ruins close to targets. The soaring Temple of Mercury was near the Al Shams.

"The President gave his approval for a retaliatory strike to be conducted on November 16," according to Robert McFarlane, Reagan's national security adviser. "It was a direct, unambiguous decision." The regional US Navy commander said he was ready and asked for the required authority to launch at first light. But that authority from the Department of Defense was never sent.

Not long after McFarlane got to the White House at 6 a.m. on November 16, he recalled, Cap Weinberger called.

"Bud," he said, "I had a request [to strike] but I denied it."

McFarlane remembered being "dumbfounded." "What went wrong?" he asked.

After some vague comments, Weinberger was blunt. "I just don't think it was the right thing to do," the defense chief said.

Outrageous, McFarlane thought. *A direct violation of a presidential order!* Such insubordination made the ex-Marine fume. The president would be upset, he told Weinberger. "I'd be glad to talk to him," Weinberger replied. McFarlane immediately took the issue to the Oval Office.

"I don't understand," Reagan said. "Why didn't they do it?"

"There is no excuse for it," McFarlane said. "You approved this operation, and Cap decided not to carry it out. The credibility of the United States in Damascus just went to zero. There's no justification. The secretary of defense was wrong, and you ought to make clear to him how you feel."

"Gosh, that's really disappointing," Reagan said. "That's terrible."

McFarlane understood Reagan's muttered misgivings as a show for his benefit. Reagan was really happy to put the crucial presidential authority to make war in the hands of Weinberger, a friend since Reagan had decided to run for governor of California 16 years earlier. To McFarlane, it was another instance where Reagan could not cope with conflicting opinions. The first duty of the chief executive was making complex decisions with ramifications that strained the mind. Reagan wanted others to make those choices. Weinberger understood that better than McFarlane. As for reprisals, the defense chief thought they did little good. The November 16 French strike on Baalbek missed all targets, according to photo reconnaissance. "The French accomplished nothing," Weinberger told reporters. "They probably made some people feel good."

Despite all of the Marine deaths, Weinberger was not channeling the hawkish inclinations of Silver Screen Six. "I'm not an eye-for-an-eye man," Weinberger said. Army General John Vessey, Chairman of the Joint Chiefs, also favored inaction, saying, "It is beneath our dignity to retaliate against the terrorist who blew up the Marine barracks." In noisy disagreement with the center of US military strength was Secretary of State George Shultz. "We cannot opt out of every contest," Shultz said. "We cannot wait for absolute certainty and clarity. If we do, the world's future will be determined by others—most likely by those who are the most brutal, the most unscrupulous and the most hostile to everything we believe in." Within Oval Office debates, Shultz told Reagan that the Pentagon was encouraging more terrorism. Without reprisals, Shultz said Reagan was showing that "terrorism works."

On February 4, 1984, Reagan once more vowed to keep Marines in Beirut in order to support the government of Lebanon. "Yes, the situation in Lebanon is difficult, frustrating, and dangerous," he said. "But that is no reason to turn our backs on friends and to cut and run. If we do, we'll be sending one signal to terrorists everywhere: They can gain by waging war against innocent people."

Three weeks later, the president decided to cut and run. Despite promising to remain in Lebanon, Reagan ordered a withdrawal three months after the Marine massacre. The final units pulled away from Green Beach at 12:47 p.m. on February 27—with the shattered barracks at their back. Some were bitter. "You have any good friends?" Lance Corporal Shawn Lamb asked one reporter. "How would you like to have them blown up in their sleep a thousand miles from home in a foreign country—for nothing?" An artillery unit staged a dawn ceremony. No bugle could be found. A small tape recorder played a scratchy cassette of the Marine Hymn. The unit's American flag was lowered and folded into a neat triangle. "Let's have a Hoo-Rah," Captain Brad Gates shouted. "Hoo-Rah," yelled the men of H Battery. In the battered Marine compound, in what had once been the commissary, a blackboard had a chalked memorial:

WELCOME TO THE "HOTEL CALIFORNIA"
You can check out, but
You can NEVER leave!!

From the looming Shuf Mountains, Druse artillery rounds landed near the Marine positions at Beirut International Airport. Most Marines were already gone, leaving at least a million green sandbags at abandoned positions. For the first time, the World War II battleship USS *New Jersey* fired its 16-inch guns at the Druse positions. A stream of fire from the gun's muzzle followed each of the 250 shells, each carrying 1,900 pounds of high explosive. Reporters and the departing Marines watched the offshore battlewagon's low-slung prow steam along in the blue Mediterranean, covering the horizon with black smoke and fire. The destroyer USS *Caron* joined in with 300 5-inch shells. There were no postbombardment reports except a Marine statement that the targets were in "Syrian-controlled Lebanon." Presumed dead but not mentioned were civilian victims of naval gunfire without forward observers. It was more of the acceptable violence common to Beirut. When the last amphibious personnel carrier was loaded, Staff Sergeant Jerry Elokonich was on top with his hands clasped overhead. "You see that surf, I'm going in it," he told reporters. "We did our job, I'll put it that way. Goodbye, folks."

Druse and Shiite Amal militia soldiers carrying their weapons showed up to watch the Marines pull away. With the Marines gone, the Amal soldiers started enforcing the Muslim edicts against alcohol at West Beirut establishments. In anticipation of their arrival the bartender at the hotel where I was staying—the Commodore—stocked the shelves with bottled water and sodas. Even so, the marauding Amal found the hidden hard stuff and smashed the bottles with their rifles. This was the bar where I met frequently with Terry Anderson, the redheaded bureau chief of the Associated Press. His office was just across the side street from the Commodore. As a former wire service reporter, I would talk with him about AP and United Press International. Terry would drink beer from a cold bottle. In almost every conversation, the ex-Marine who served two tours in Vietnam would rank Beirut number one on the chaos list. "This is a nut house," Terry said. He played tennis almost every morning, so it was easy for Imad Mughniyeh and his Hezbollah militia henchmen to track Anderson. On March 16, 1985, they snatched Anderson leaving the court and dumped him in the trunk of a car. For the next six years, Anderson was never sure where he was being held prisoner. At one point, he thought he heard the last gasps of William Buckley, the Central Intelligence Agency officer Mughniyeh had also grabbed off the streets of Beirut. He shared hovels with six other American hostages. Most of the hostages of the Iranian-backed Mughniyeh were held in inhumane conditions, chained to radiators and taken outside only when moved to different locations.

With the Marines dead and gone, Iran's Shiite militia in Baalbek became Reagan's recurring nightmare. In addition to the collection of American, French, and British hostages, Mughniyeh's Hezbollah gunmen continued to flout American interests. On orders from Iran, Mughniyeh hijacked Trans World Airlines (TWA) Flight 847 in Athens on June 14, 1985. The hijackers, Hassan Izz-al-Din and Muhammad Ali Hamadi, began searching the American plane for US servicemen. They soon discovered a group of Navy divers, including Robert Stethem, 23, from Waterbury, Connecticut. One of the hijackers shot Stethem through the temple. During the 17-day ordeal televised around the world, the hijackers flew to Beirut, Algiers, and then back to Beirut. In front of the media cameras, the hijackers threw Stethem's dead body from the plane and shot him again. Reagan seemed helpless in the face of reporters' questions.

Q: What's the plan?

The President: You know that I couldn't answer that question or tell you. I don't think we could make things like that public.

Q: Are you ruling out military deterrence, sir?

The President: Yes.

Reagan was starting to appear more pliable with the terrorists than the man he castigated for weakness almost daily in 1980—Jimmy Carter. The headline on one critical editorial read "Jimmy Reagan."

A brazen Mughniyeh himself joined the hijackers in the TWA jetliner in Beirut, proof to US intelligence that Tehran was in control of events. An engine failed on landing in Beirut, forcing Mughniyeh to cancel plans to take the plane and its passengers to Tehran. Meanwhile, Reagan secretly agreed to one demand by Mughniyeh:

Israel must release 700 Shiites seized in Lebanon. It was a back-room deal worked out with Israeli prime minister Yitzak Rabin by Secretary of State George Shultz. Reagan sought to portray Syrian president Hafez al-Assad as the man behind the TWA hijacking and kidnapping of passengers. Washington was negotiating the passengers' fate with the more moderate Shiite militia, Amal, headed by Nabih Berri. When passengers were removed from the plane they were moved to Damascus, four were taken by Mughniyeh's Hezbolla. Suddenly, the release of the hostages Reagan was hoping for was unsettled. Assad sought a solution by inviting Hashemi Rafsanjani, the speaker of the Iranian parliament, to Damascus for negotiations. Under pressure from Assad, the Iranians released the four passengers. Although American diplomats and intelligence officials knew of Iran's dominant role in the TWA hijacking, Reagan made no mention of Tehran's participation. Instead, he sought to make the Syrian president the bad guy.

What was to be a diplomatic thank-you for having the TWA passengers released in Damascus turned into a one-sided tirade. Reagan fired insults at Assad during the phone call. Assad knew where the hijackers were—it was plain murder, Reagan said. He didn't want to hear how the hijackers vanished in Beirut.

Every time Assad tried to speak, Reagan cut him off. Reagan demanded Assad produce Terry Anderson and the six other hostages under control of Iran's Hezbollah militia and Imad Mughniyeh. Assad never got a chance to answer. Reagan slammed down the White House phone.

Reagan had a far more civil tone when his government started asking the ayatollahs of Iran to return the seven hostages.

14

End of an Era

Clouds hid the stars so the night was all murk, and the back canyon road was treacherous. Ronald Wilson Reagan and his wife, Nancy, were low on gas and uncertain, even lost. On the next turn, Reagan spotted a light in a ranch house. He was greeted at the door and instantly recognized. "Say," the rancher said, "I know you! Tell me your name." "Well," Reagan said, smiling, "I will just tell you my initials—RR." "Wow," said the rancher. "Is your wife with you?" "Waiting in the car," Reagan replied. With that, the rancher called upstairs: "Ma, come down. Roy Rogers is here! And Dale Evans is with him!"
—ANECDOTE FROM RONALD REAGAN'S 1976, CAMPAIGN

Reagan's strongest attribute was his ability to make listeners laugh. Every Reagan audience during the 1976 presidential campaign would roar at the *RR* story or ones like it. As he often did, Reagan was poking fun at himself. Sure, he was a Hollywood actor, but never on the level of a Roy Rogers. Roy Rogers would be something to yell about. Roy Rogers was King of the Cowboys. He could ride and shoot with his white Stetson bending in the breeze and a bandanna streaming from his throat. His noble steed was Trigger, a golden palomino, ears laid back, four hooves in the air, and a tail full and flowing like a silver banner. Gabby Hayes, mumbling through his nose and white whiskers, made you chuckle. Dale always sang along with Roy in the slower parts of almost a hundred movies and weekly television shows. And the cowboy quartet, Sons of the Pioneers, singing of two lost wranglers tortured by a desert mirage.

> *He's a devil not a man*
> *And he spreads the burning sands*

When movies were a nickel in the 1940s, Roy and his troupe became part of American culture. Every Saturday afternoon generations of kids would gallop out of the theaters on an imaginary Trigger. And they would flock to the fairgrounds when Roy was on tour with Trigger, splattering mudballs in midair with his Colt. Roy Rogers was big. To this day, *The Roy Rogers Show* is broadcast on cable television.

No, Ronald Reagan was not a star. In 1976, he had been out of film and television for a dozen years. Older folks might recall him searching for his missing legs in *Kings Row*. Some saw him on television's *GE Theater*. Still, the laughter took the edge off those in the crowd ready to dismiss and disbelieve Reagan as a B-movie actor.

A good sense of humor, voters thought. *Wasn't he governor of California?*

With laughter, we sucked in oxygen, stimulating the heart and the lungs. Endorphins are released in the brain. With improved circulation, muscles relax. Stress ebbs. "A good, relaxed feeling," says the Mayo Clinic in listing the physical and psychological benefits of laughter. Even inexperienced public speakers know that telling a joke is a great way to start.

Reagan's use of laughter made him one of the most formidable American politicians of his day. From the outset of his career in 1966, the joke was the biggest in his toolbox. "He liked to leave them laughing," said Caspar Weinberger, who was with him at the outset. What those crowds were getting was something far more than an aging actor. Reagan used his professional skills to enthrall voters and engineer astounding political feats.

In 1976, Reagan started to become even bigger than Roy Rogers. Against a sitting Republican president with all the political accouterments of White House power, Reagan waged a primary campaign that sometimes defied belief. Take the 1976 presidential primary in Texas. Reagan carried every county—all 254. It was a front-page shocking defeat of President Gerald R. Ford. Even after Air Force One and the presidential limousine visited the Republican state convention in Rolla, Missouri, Reagan swept the delegates; Ford's local woman leader began sobbing as Reagan's majority mounted. At the Kansas City National Republican Convention that year, Reagan came within 17 delegates of wresting the nomination from Ford. And he did it mostly with a warm and friendly manner before crowds big and small, with rarely a harsh word for his opponent. In public or private, Reagan's manners were impeccable. Every speech was a production. Suits—even the brown ones—were tailored to emphasize broad shoulders. Weights, push-ups, and pull-ups gave him a leading-man torso. When surgeons sought to remove an assassin's bullet in 1981, it took 40 minutes to cut through chest muscle blocking their access. Undyed chestnut hair that drooped below his nose was coated with Brylcreem and molded into a pompadour that crested a collection of hills and swales around his ears. His complexion was so rosy that some suspected rouge. It was just that Hollywood glow. The actor's posture made his six-foot-one seem closer to six-foot-four. The gaze was direct except for the tilt to the left with a bashful, disarming grin. Contacts overcame terrible vision. Hearing aids and lip reading also compensated for the infirmities of old age. Even for a handful of voters, the sound system's mike seemed always perfectly tuned to amplify a clear, calm tenor. The voice was often booked by Hollywood directors no longer interested in his face. They wanted the perfect voice-over narration. The rhythm of speech flowed until a delay of two beats—just before the rancher yelled the punch line about Roy Rogers—were evidence of endless rehearsals. Cryptic notes—he used coded abbreviations—on a stack of soiled 3" × 5" cards prompted lines honed by decades on what Reagan called the rubber-chicken circuit. He spilled those cards to the platform floor during one event. It was akin to a teleprompter going haywire for today's politicians. Hastily rearranged, the cards threw Reagan out of sync. Punch lines came before the setup. "I'm getting ahead of myself," he apologized. That was a rare mishap. With only notes on the cards, Reagan's speeches would enter the minds, the hearts, and the souls of the faithful and enlist them to his cause. Oh, he did Republican dog whistles for blacks and the poor.

"Doesn't it make you angry when you see a strapping young buck ahead of you in the checkout line using food stamps?" he asked at a Florida rally. In speech after speech, he deplored welfare cheats. "In Chicago, they found a woman who holds the record," Reagan said. "She used 80 names, 30 addresses, 15 telephone numbers to collect food stamps, Social Security, veterans' benefits for four nonexistent deceased veteran husbands, as well as welfare. Her tax-free cash income alone has been running $150,000 a year." Some gasped. Others shook their heads. It was part of Reagan's relentless assault on the very governments he would lead, Sacramento and Washington. As a spokesman for General Electric, Reagan articulated the corporate assault on taxes, big government, and federal safety and air pollution regulations. Social Security, Reagan said, was nothing but a welfare program. To him, Medicare was socialized medicine. Even so, Reagan's mellifluousness seemed to remove the sting of his remarks' inherent meanness toward the elderly and the ill. He took the edge off the hostility of the Republican right wing. Instead of disapproving of the hooded racism, voters tended to enjoy the performance. In 1980, he was the first presidential candidate to ask how you could spot the Pole at a cockfight. "He's the one with the duck," Reagan answered with a smile. How can you spot the Italian? "He's the one that bets on the duck." How do you know the Mafia is there? "The duck wins," Reagan said. Such ethnic jokes can be political poison, but Reagan defiantly repeated it for television reporters.

For all his hard-right baggage, Reagan was surprisingly mild on the stump. In his 1980 battle with President Jimmy Carter, Reagan was portrayed as an irresponsible ideologue who could get the United States into a nuclear war with the Soviet Union. At the time, Carter's reelection bid was saddled with soaring inflation, double-digit interest rates, and pain at the neighborhood filling station. "I will accept being irresponsible," Reagan said, "if President Carter accepts being responsible." In another exchange, a reporter challenged Reagan's recurring charge that Democrats were responsible for budget deficits and the national debt. Aren't you responsible as well? the reporter asked. "Yes, I too am responsible," Reagan said. "I was a Democrat for many years."

For Reagan, evoking laughter was a skill that tapped a human instinct so basic that it crossed both political and international boundaries. A 10-year study by Robert Provine found that laughter is a universal human vocabulary recognized by people of all cultures. "We somehow laugh at just the right times, without consciously knowing why we do it," Provine wrote in 2001. "Laughter is primarily a social vocalization that binds people together. . . . It is not a learned group reaction but an instinctive behavior programmed by our genes. Laughter bonds us through humor and play."

Something like that happened on March 30, 1981, just two months after Reagan's inauguration. That day, his knees buckled and his eyes rolled back at the entrance to George Washington University Medical Center as he fainted from the effects of John Hinckley's .22 caliber Röhm RG-14 pistol. One of the six bullets Hinckley fired shattered on the armor plating of the presidential limousine door. A ricocheting fragment entered below Reagan's left armpit, punctured a lung, bounced off a rib, and came to rest three inches from his heart. "Honey, I forgot to duck," Reagan messaged Nancy before being wheeled into the operating room. Before anesthesia, Reagan looked at the surgical team. "Please tell me you're Republicans," he said. These one-liners were fed to reporters while surgeons were still digging for the bullet fragment. Other gags followed. His mouth clogged with tubes, Reagan scribbled them out in the recovery room. "I'd like to do this scene again," said one note. "Send me to L.A. where I can see the air I'm breathing."

His three top advisers arrived at his bedside. The White House was running smoothly without him, said one. "What makes you think I'm happy about that," Reagan wrote.

The global shock wave of the attempted assassination was quickly tempered by almost universal smiles and admiration for Reagan's bravado in the face of death. Mike Deaver, who had been molding Reagan's image since his first days as a politician, was in the middle of the shooting. When Hinckley fired, Deaver ducked and then hit the ground outside the rear entrance of the Washington Hilton. At the hospital, it was Deaver who checked the bleeding president in with an intern holding a clipboard. R-E-A-G-A-N, Deaver spelled. First name? Ron. Address? 1600 Pennsylvania Avenue. "His pencil stopped in mid-scratch," Deaver said. "He finally looked up. 'You mean ... ?'" Deaver, in charge of all pageantry affecting the president's approval rating, was quick to grasp the impact of the day's events. Looking back years later, Deaver viewed the turmoil and the jokes as the seminal moment for the fortieth president. "The popularity of Ronald Reagan, the remarkable acceptance of at least the first six years of his presidency, began to take shape that day, driven by his grace and aplomb under circumstances hard to conceive," Deaver recalled.

Laughter bailed Reagan out of one of his worst moments as president. It happened as he sought reelection in 1984 during a second debate with the Democratic candidate, former vice president Walter Mondale. In their first meeting, the 56-year-old Mondale seemed sharper and quicker. The 73-year-old Reagan was slow, fumbled facts, and was declared the loser by even the Republican media. To Speaker Tip O'Neill, Reagan was just running to form.

"Many people were shocked by how poorly the president performed during the first debate, in the 1984 campaign, but to me, that was the real Reagan," the Boston congressman said. "Reagan lacked the knowledge he should have in every sphere, both domestic and international. Most of the time he was an actor reading lines, who didn't understand his own program. I hate to say it about such an agreeable man, but it was sinful that Reagan ever became president."

Speculation focused on damage caused by the attempted assassination three years earlier. Polls showed Mondale had cut into Reagan's lead but was still behind. For their second debate, in Kansas City, Mondale laid the 1983 Marine massacre at Reagan's podium. Through slick media manipulation, the White House had hidden Reagan's culpability in the Marine disaster. Using new facts from a *Nation* magazine article, Mondale drew a portrait of presidential incompetence and miscalculation that led to the Beirut massacre of 220 Marines, 18 sailors, and three Army enlisted men. Reagan's support of Israel's 1982 invasion of Lebanon resulted in a series of US disasters in 1983 including the single biggest Marine death toll since Iwo Jima in World War II. Mondale punched relentlessly with the facts: Despite repeated pleas, Reagan refused to move the Marines to safety aboard ships offshore in Beirut. Because the Marines were indefensible, both Defense Secretary Caspar Weinberger and the Joint Chiefs of Staff urged Reagan to withdraw a week before the terrorist attack.

"They went to him five days before they were killed and said, 'Please, take them out of there.' . . . He did not do so," Mondale said. Reagan refused to join in retaliatory air strikes on the terrorist targets by France and Israel, who also suffered troop losses. "The President told the terrorists he was going to retaliate. He didn't. They called [his] bluff. And the bottom line is that the United States left in humiliation, and our enemies are stronger," Mondale said. The Mondale assault was reinforced by columnist Morton Kondracke, one of the panelists questioning the debaters. He included the Americans killed when the US embassy was destroyed by the same terrorists six months before the Marines were slaughtered.

"Mr. President, four years ago you criticized President Carter for ignoring ample warnings that our diplomats in Iran might be taken hostage," Kondracke said. "Haven't you done exactly the same thing in Lebanon, not once, but three times, with 300 Americans, not hostages, but dead? And you vowed swift retaliation against terrorists, but doesn't our lack of response suggest that you're just bluffing?"

French and Israeli forces were also bombed during the same period. They staged fighter-bomber reprisals on terrorist camps, but Reagan refused to join the retaliation. His refusal to unleash Navy carrier warplanes off the coast of Lebanon caused widespread and public anger among the surviving Marines in Beirut.

"The president is called the Commander in Chief," Mondale said. "He's called that because he's supposed to be in charge." Mondale's pummeling had clearly wounded Reagan. "As Groucho Marx said: 'Who do you believe? Me or your own eyes?'" Mondale said.

Reagan's response reflected more panic than rehearsal.

Throughout his political career, he repeatedly sought to identify himself with the sacrifice of military heroism. In his inaugural address in 1981, he singled out the bravery of a dead Army messenger and listed the famous battlefields from Belleau Wood to the jungles of Vietnam. He gestured to Arlington Cemetery across the Potomac with its rows of white crosses and the Stars of David. "They add up to only a tiny fraction of the price that has been paid for our freedom," Reagan said. Suddenly, in the heat of the debate with Mondale, Reagan abandoned his responsibility as commander in chief. He turned the sacrifice of 241 young men—21 are buried in Section 59 in Arlington—into military bungling.

Moderator Edwin Newman asked: "Your rebuttal, Mr. President?"

Reagan slyly shifted the issue from the pleas for a timely withdrawal to the barracks where the 241 were sleeping. "Yes. First of all, Mr. Mondale should know that the President of the United States did not order the Marines into that barracks. That was a command decision made by the commanders on the spot and based with what they thought was best for the men there."

For Silver Screen Six, the words were somewhere between dastardly and despicable. Before a watching nation, Reagan singled out—not by name—the commander of the 24th Marine Amphibious Unit. That was Colonel Timothy Joseph Geraghty, who had already suffered all the humiliations the Marine Corps and Department of Defense could assemble. Reagan knew better than most that Geraghty had been ordered to violate almost every military edict to comply with the White House's dubious, conflicting, and shifting policies. Reagan had made the Marines take the low ground in Beirut. When they started to be killed by snipers on the hills above, Reagan secretly telephoned Geraghty in Beirut. He promised presidential support—"whatever support it takes to stop the attacks," Reagan pledged—and ordered Geraghty to use air and sea power against Muslim forces despite the colonel's objections that it would lead to slaughter for his Marines. Construction of better defensive positions by Navy Seabee crews was denied. To minimize artillery attacks on Marines in outlying foxholes on weekends, Geraghty moved most of them into the concrete and steel Battalion Landing Team quarters where so many died. As he was still hunting body parts of the 241 dead, Geraghty realized that he—not Reagan—would take the blame. That night, Reagan made sure Geraghty took the fall on prime time.

To *Washington Post* columnist Mary McGrory, the escaping of responsibility showed Reagan's ruthlessness.

"He does what he has to do to survive, even if it means contradicting himself and history," McGrory wrote. "He has the true killer instinct, as he demonstrated when he meanly put the blame for the Beirut massacre on the ground commanders. In his most reprehensible moment, he defended himself at the expense of Marine officers, who were following his orders and trying to carry out the murky mission he gave them."

In the presidential debate, Reagan sought to escape the results of his earliest decisions as president-elect. Reagan and his most senior advisers were lightweights, uninterested in and largely ignorant of the world outside the United States. His entire foreign policy was based on unrelenting attacks on the Soviet Union, which was already in steep decline and headed for collapse. Reagan's untutored national security team produced a series of fiascos and disasters.

Mondale sought to portray Reagan as irresponsible and incompetent. "I want to quote . . . Harry Truman," said Mondale. "He said, 'The buck stops here.' . . . Who's in charge? Who's handling this matter? That's my main point." It was clearly the most dramatic part of the presidential debate.

As in the first debate, Mondale was ahead on points. Was Reagan, then 73, too old for a second term? The issue was raised by Hank Trewhitt of *The Baltimore Sun*. "You already are the oldest president in history," Trewhitt noted, "and some of your staff say you were tired after your most recent encounter with Mr. Mondale. Is there any doubt in your mind that you would be able to function?"

It was the slow curve Reagan was waiting for. "I will not make age an issue of this campaign," Reagan said. "I am not going to exploit, for political purposes, my opponent's youth and inexperience." Mondale shook with laughter. The audience roared. Millions watching on television joined in. It was the instant highlight for network news reports, where editors repeated the clip for days. America's dean of political reporting, David Broder, dismissed the Reagan culpability in Beirut. In *The Washington Post,* Broder focused on how Reagan laughed away fears that he was addled by age. "He delivered the perfect rejoinder," Broder wrote. Once again Reagan had left them laughing. And once more the Marines were buried lower in national reporting.

Two weeks later, Reagan won voters in 49 states, leaving Mondale only his home state of Minnesota and the District of Columbia. It was his second straight landslide victory.

Ronald Reagan and Thomas P. O'Neill were political archenemies. But you wouldn't know it when the Republican president and Democratic Speaker of the House started swapping stories.

It was a tragedy at the brewery. Michael O'Brien tumbled from the rafters into a vat of Guinness and drowned. Mrs. O'Brien shrieked at the news. "Oh, Michael! He couldn't swim. Not a stroke. He had no chance." The brewery manager paused as her tears flowed. "Well, Mrs. O'Brien, he did have a chance," he said. "He came out twice to pee."

That was just one Reagan exchanged with Tip O'Neill, who represented North Boston but controlled power that often exceeded that of the president of the United States. Any laws the new president might have in mind would have to pass through the fingers of the silver-haired soldier of the New Deal. O'Neill slaved for Franklin Delano Roosevelt, Harry S. Truman, John F. Kennedy, Lyndon B. Johnson, and Jimmy Carter. As a defecting Democrat, Reagan was a traitor to O'Neill's cause. Tip O'Neill's disdain for the Reagan agenda could be seen in the early banishment from the Speaker's Lobby of White House lobbyist Max Friedersdorf. So Friedersdorf expected a cool, even tense initial private meeting between O'Neill and Reagan at the White House family quarters. Drinks loosened both men. In adult life, Reagan limited himself to just one—orange juice and vodka. O'Neill had no such restrictions. The laughter began. "It was just hilarious," Friedersdorf said. O'Neill "had a real repertoire of jokes, but each one he would tell, Reagan would come right back—just two old Irishmen—and top his story." The night ended with warm exchanges between Tip and Ron.

The depth of O'Neill's affection for Reagan would be on display after Reagan was shot. In the hospital room, where Reagan was still sedated, O'Neill went to his knees and held the president's hand. "The Lord is my shepherd; I shall not want," O'Neill prayed. "He maketh me to lie down in green pastures: he leadeth me beside the still waters. He restoreth my soul: he leadeth me in the paths of righteousness for his name's sake. Yea, though I walk through the valley of the shadow of death, I will fear no evil, for thou art with me; thy rod and thy staff they comfort me."

Two days later O'Neill returned with a gift—a book of Irish humor. "I was shocked by his condition," O'Neill said. "This was three days after the shooting. I suspect that in the first day or two he was probably closer to death than most of us realized. If he hadn't been so strong and hardy, it could have been all over."

Their relationship began on Inauguration Day 1981, when Reagan slipped into the Speaker's office at the Capitol to change from formal wear to street clothes. The new president admired O'Neill's desk. It once belonged to President Grover Cleveland, O'Neill said. "That's very interesting," Reagan said. "You know, I once played Grover Cleveland in the movies." No, O'Neill reminded him, you played the baseball pitcher Grover Cleveland Alexander. O'Neill had seen the old Reagan movie a month earlier. O'Neill was a television viewer in the evenings, and in the 1950s he and his wife, Millie, used to watch Reagan as host of GE Theater. When the Speaker tried to explain to the president the importance of chemistry with Congress, Reagan's eyes seemed glazed. "I could have been speaking Latin for all he seemed to care," O'Neill said. Yet Reagan's White House team was adept at pushing an agenda of tax breaks, as well as cuts in welfare and education programs that O'Neill had spent a lifetime building. "Even with our many intense political battles we managed to maintain a pretty good friendship," O'Neill said.

Over the next six years, O'Neill and Reagan had a love-hate relationship. More than once Speaker O'Neill quelled his Democratic majority to protect Reagan during the darkest moments of his presidency. When Democrats were demanding enforcement of the War Powers Act when Marines came under fire in 1983, O'Neill worked out a compromise.

One of the most effective Democratic opponents on the Marine deployment was Congressman Sam Gibbons of Florida, a World War II veteran who had parachuted into Normandy on D-day in 1945. "If we are there to fight, we are far too few," Gibbons told the House. "If we are there to die, we are far too many."

Instead of an embarrassing forced withdrawal of the Marines embattled in Beirut, there was a narrow agreement engineered by O'Neill to extend their stay for 18 months. O'Neill was elected Speaker in part because of his opposition to the Vietnam War. In supporting Reagan, O'Neill argued that bipartisan support on foreign policy was best for the nation. A majority of Democrats voted against their leader, but enough Republicans made up the difference. The Democratic Speaker, ostensibly the archenemy, saved the Republican president from humiliation.

For Reagan, in the year following reelection in 1984, his personal performance overcame any setbacks abroad or with Congress. According to Gallup voter surveys, Reagan was astounding. "Reagan continued to soar in 1985, routinely receiving [approval] ratings in the 60% range," Gallup reported. "In May 1986, Reagan received a 68% job approval rating—tied for the highest of his administration." Suddenly, five months later, Reagan's rating suffered a 16-point drop. The slide was precipitated by a few lines that appeared on the bottom of page 11 in *Al-Shiraa*, a Beirut newspaper that specialized in events in Tehran. On November 3, 1986, *Al-Shiraa* reported, "A secret U.S. envoy, Robert McFarlane, visited Tehran secretly" and conducted extremely important talks with the Foreign Ministry, the Consultative Assembly, and the army. This resulted in a deal that brought four American planes "carrying spare parts" for Iran's air defenses in its six-year-old war with President Saddam Hussein and Iraq. "These contributed to a large extent of improving the Iranian air defense system which last week downed three Iraqi planes, one a Sokhoi and two MiG23a." That blurb ripped the cover off Reagan's $50 million ransom attempt to free seven Americans held by the Iranian-controlled Hezbollah militia. The president supplied Iran with Hawk antiaircraft systems and 2,004 tank-killing TOW missiles. Only three hostages were released. And six more were captured. They were held by Iran's Hezbollah in Baalbek, the "terrorists" who blew up the US embassy in Beirut and bombed the Marine barracks—the very same terrorists Reagan had vowed to destroy. The revelations opened a wound in Reagan's presidency that would bleed for two years.

While the *Al-Shiraa* report had few details, it was enough to produce such hysteria at the White House that 10 days later, on November 13, 1986, a rattled President Reagan looked Americans in
the eye during a nationwide broadcast to refute charges that he said
were "utterly false." "You're going to hear the facts from a White
House source, and you know my name," Regan began. As professional actors often have to do, he read lines that turned out to be
preposterous—a series of distortions, twisted facts, and tortured
logic that instantly achieved an historic status in presidential speech
annals. The whopper came early on, when Reagan said, "For 18
months now we have had underway a secret diplomatic initiative
to Iran. That initiative was undertaken for the simplest and best of
reasons: to renew a relationship with the nation of Iran, to bring an
honorable end to the bloody 6-year war between Iran and Iraq." He
did add "and to effect the safe return of all hostages." But if anything, the new American weapons were to bolster Iran's battlefield
prowess against Iraq in that bloody six-year war. At a news conference a week later, Reagan had to deal with a crush of facts showing
he shipped arms to Iran in hopes of the release of hostages. It was so
bad, reporters suggested he quit dodging the truth.

Q: What would be wrong in saying that a mistake was made
on a very high-risk gamble so that you can get on with the next
two years?

The President: Because I don't think a mistake was made. It
was a high-risk gamble, and it was a gamble that, as I've said, I believe the circumstances warranted. And I don't see that it has been
a fiasco or a great failure of any kind. . . . We got our hostages
back—three of them.

A *Los Angeles Times* poll showed only 14 percent of those surveyed believed the president.

The level of lying by Reagan in that first speech reflected an unskilled and untutored writer with the integrity of a pirate. Patrick Buchanan, a longtime Republican hatchet man, did the final draft, according to Reagan Presidential Library records. But the detailed content was the work of two brilliant and accomplished men—John Poindexter and Donald Regan. Poindexter, top of his class at Annapolis, was an admiral in the US Navy and Reagan's fourth national security adviser. Regan, White House chief of staff, prevailed in the rough world of Wall Street to make millions and direct the fortunes of Merrill Lynch stockbrokers. But both were political nitwits. They were convinced Reagan could talk his way out of a scandal that had more legs than a centipede. They had conned the president into a stonewall defense. Shultz recalled one meeting where he condemned every aspect of the hostage recovery with realistic facts.

"The president was unmoved by my words," Shultz said. "The president was in a steamy, angry mood clearly directed at me: get off my back. He was angry in a way I had never seen before. Ronald Reagan pounded the table. 'We are right!' he said. 'We had to take the opportunity! And we were successful! History will never forgive us if we don't do this! And no one will talk about it.'"

But eventually, everyone did talk. That one Reagan speech turned out to be the launchpad for four separate Washington investigations and a special prosecutor who produced 11 indictments that would accuse five senior Reagan administration officials of criminal wrongdoing—Defense Secretary Weinberger, Admiral Poindexter, Assistant Secretary of State Eliott Abrams, Robert McFarlane, and Marine Major Oliver North. All escaped jail with a presidential pardon from Reagan's successor, President George H. W. Bush. As Reagan's vice president, Bush had endorsed the plot. A federal court overruled North's conviction.

McFarlane, Reagan's third national security adviser, was blamed as the father of the fiasco. Once more, he was striving to follow in the footsteps of his mentor, Henry Kissinger. McFarlane would later argue that overtures from "moderates" in Iran led him to reestablish ties with the government of Ayatollah Ruhollah Khomeini. To ignore Tehran "would be have been as grave a mistake as ignoring Chinese overtures to reestablish relations in the 1970s."

McFarlane was harking back to his time as a military aide to Kissinger, who became celebrated for secret missions to Beijing that led to President Richard Nixon's historic trip to China. But a closer look shows it was Nixon—not Beijing and not Kissinger—who initiated the resumption of diplomatic relations. McFarlane's hero was in fact opposed to Nixon's outreach to China. According to Alexander Haig, Kissinger thought Nixon mad. During the second week of Nixon's administration, Haig was the top assistant to National Security Adviser Kissinger.

"Henry came back from the Oval Office and said to me, 'Al, this madman wants to normalize our relations with China.' And he laughed. And I said, 'Oh my God.'"

A secret mission to Tehran had become an obsession with McFarlane. He had resigned his White House post but pushed Reagan for the Iranian opening. It worried Secretary of State Schultz. "Bud was always tempted to go off on a 'secret mission' and negotiate backroom deals," Shultz said. "He seemed to want to pull off something akin to a Henry Kissinger–China deal." Shultz and Defense Secretary Weinberger were the most vehement opponents of McFarlane's scheme once it was put on paper. The "overtures" from

Iran were in fact proposals from Israel, which had had a thriving arms trade with Iran for decades. But the trade had ebbed after the United States made aggressive efforts to cut off arms supplies to Iran in 1983. Shultz led an effort to freeze shipments to Iran from the always-thriving weapons black market between nations. It was Israel who assured McFarlane that the seven US hostages would be released once American arms reached the Tehran government— an assurance that McFarlane quickly gave to Reagan. McFarlane's "contact" with Tehran was, Manucher Ghorbanifar. He had been an Iranian intelligence agent under the shah but was strictly an arms dealer when McFarlane met him. It was a replay of McFarlane being taken in during the 1980 Reagan presidential campaign by an Iranian who promised to engineer the release of US embassy hostages in Tehran. Ghorbanifar had been such a river of lies and betrayals in the backroom of intelligence that the Central Intelligence Agency had singled him out for a "Burn Notice"—do not touch. Ghorbanifar handled the details of the weapon sales to Iran and, in most cases, doubled the original $50 million price tag. Despite promises of freedom, only two of the seven hostages were released. And six more Americans were grabbed from the streets of Beirut. Meanwhile, Ghorbanifar sold 1,408 TOW missiles to Iran in 1985.

Ghorbanifar paved the way for—at last—McFarlane's secret mission in May of 1986. When Kissinger slipped into Beijing in 1971, Zhou Enlai and other leaders greeted him as a VIP with a series of elaborate dinners. In Tehran, no one showed up to greet the secret emissary from the president of the United States. McFarlane sat in the Tehran airport waiting room for two hours.

"This was, of course, the first bad omen," McFarlane said.

It was the first of a series. Ghorbanifar finally showed up and took the unofficial party in two beat-up cars to a rundown hotel, where he and McFarlane had a quick exchange. McFarlane asked when he would meet with the prime minister and the speaker of the Iranian parliament. "It wasn't clear," Ghorbanifar said. Another bad omen.

"The alarm bells went off in my mind," McFarlane said. He had been duped. Instead of senior officials who could talk about an eventual reestablishment of relations with the United State— the opening—there were only rude bureaucrats, "led by a strident young functionary who insisted there had been no prior commitment to release the hostages and launched into repeated diatribes for not having brought enough Hawk spare parts," McFarlane said. On his plane from Israel, McFarlane carried 240 spares for the antiaircraft Hawk system. Only after hostages were released were the parts to be transferred. But the Iranians grabbed the cargo shortly after his plane landed. "To my chagrin," McFarlane said. Another 1,000 TOW missiles were shipped later.

It was North who provided the highlights of the trip. He delivered an Israeli-baked chocolate cake in the shape of a key, to symbolize the unlocking of US-Iranian relations, and a bible Reagan signed and inscribed from Galatians 3:8. "All the nations shall be blessed in you." According to McFarlane, it was on that trip that North first alluded to using money from the arms sales to finance the president's pet project—the right-wing Contra guerrillas trying to overthrow the left-wing Sandinista government of Nicaragua. Reagan had been financing them throughout his presidency, despite prohibitions from the Democratic Congress. North got a $15 million kickback from Ghorbanifar that was later funneled to the Contras.

As details of the disastrous trip leaked, the cake and the bible added a bizarre, even silly twist. McFarlane found it increasingly hard to cope with the ridicule of what he planned to be an historic mission. "I believed the Iran-Contra scandal, which had in the last three months all but engulfed the Reagan administration, and by extension the country, was all my fault," he later wrote. He swallowed 30 Valium in hopes of dying but survived what friends later said was only a "cry for help." To McFarlane, his survival marked another failure.

As Nixon was the instigator with China, Reagan was the real instigator of Iran-Contra. It had little to do with moderates or overtures from Iran. That was merely a cloak of rationality contrived by McFarlane. What drove Reagan was the hostage families' gushing emotions that almost drowned him. In a series of 1985 meetings with the families, Reagan was challenged about his refusal to negotiate with terrorists. At a White House session, Terry Anderson's sister Peggy Say made a fiery appeal to Reagan. At the end of another meeting in Chicago Heights, Illinois, Reagan was choked and teary.

After months of silence, Reagan offered something close to the truth in a March 4, 1987, broadcast to the nation.

"A few months ago I told the American people I did not trade arms for hostages. My heart and my best intentions still tell me that's true, but the facts and the evidence tell me it is not. . . . What began as a strategic opening to Iran deteriorated, in its implementation, into trading arms for hostages. This runs counter to my own beliefs, to administration policy, and to the original strategy we had in mind. There are reasons why it happened, but no excuses. It was a mistake. . . .

"I let my personal concern for the hostages spill over into the geopolitical strategy of reaching out to Iran. I asked so many questions about the hostages' welfare that I didn't ask enough about the specifics of the total Iran plan. Let me say to the hostage families: We have not given up. We never will. And I promise you we'll use every legitimate means to free your loved ones from captivity." My colleague, Terry Anderson, was not unchained until December 4, 1991; he had been the last hostage captured, on March 16, 1985, after a tennis match in Beirut.

Reagan told the nation he had learned from his mistakes. "Now, what should happen when you make a mistake is this: You take your knocks, you learn your lessons, and then you move on. That's the healthiest way to deal with a problem." That was enough for the Democratic Congress. Impeachment was discussed by the new Speaker, Jim Wright of Texas. But Watergate and Nixon's resignation smeared the body politic in Washington, not just the Republicans. And a series of Iran-Contra investigations seemingly unearthed all the dirt. Declassified documents trickled out a series of Presidential Directives showing Reagan's signature on all the worst decisions. But there was no appetite for impeachment. "We just decided not to do it," said House Majority Leader Thomas Foley.

It was Richard Nixon who noted a crucial aspect of American politics. He was tape-recorded during a session with aides moaning about the lasting effects of Watergate: Voters quickly forget, Nixon said. Reagan's popularity improved during his final year in office. Just before he left office, Gallup reported 63 percent of those interviewed approved of the president.

January 18, 1989—two days before his second term ended—was particularly pleasant for Reagan. He welcomed to the White House the college football national champions, the University of Notre Dame. The players presented him with a sweater that had belonged to Fighting Irish football great George Gipp—the role Reagan played in the 1940 film *Knute Rockne, All American*. Almost every reporter in Washington referred to the president as "the Gipper."

The Notre Dame football team provided the ideal audience for Reagan to repeat an anecdote about the famous coach that he had used a year earlier at a fundraising reception for Pete Dawkins of New Jersey.

"Knute liked ... spirit in his ballplayers ... ," Reagan said. "Once when he was working with the four backfield stars who became known as the Four Horsemen, the fellow named Jimmy Crowley just couldn't get it right on one play. . . . Rockne, who, by the way, was Norwegian, but was commonly called the Swede—he finally got irritated after Crowley muffed a play again and hollered, 'What's dumber than a dumb Irishman?' And without missing a beat, Crowley said, 'A smart Swede.'"

The White House Rose Garden echoed with laughter.

EPILOGUE

A line of Seahorse helicopters lifted off from Chu Lai and roared over the white sand beaches and the blue surf of the South China Sea. Inside one of the helicopters was Lance Corporal Ray Hildreth, a member of the 1st Platoon, Charlie Company, of the 1st Marine Division's Reconnaissance Battalion. As the chopper swung north-west, Hildreth marveled at the beauty of Vietnam. The endless rice paddies and the hillsides were a blaze of green. The golden rays of the sun faded to purple in the dusk. *Enchanting,* Hildreth thought. Over the ridgeline of the Hiep Duc Valley, the Seahorses circled a 1,500-foot mountain marked Hill 488 on their maps. Hovering behind an outcropping that hid them from the twinkling lights in the village below, Hildreth and 14 others in the 1st Platoon dropped behind enemy lines. Also scrambling out of the helicopters were two US Navy medical corpsmen. This was a recon team, Marines often considered the elite of light infantry. Unseen from the top of Hill 488, the 15 men of 1st Platoon would direct death and destruction to the Viet Cong and the North Vietnamese regular army in the village below. Then the recon team would slip off Hill 488 in their Seahorses before the dinks knew what hit them.

The plan was worked out by Staff Sergeant Jimmie Earl Howard. "The men like him," said Captain Timothy J. Geraghty, the company commander who put Howard in charge. On June 13, 1966, the day the 1st Platoon landed, Howard had been a Marine for 16 years. He left Iowa State and its football team in 1950 and went to war in Korea. There he won a Silver Star and three Purple Hearts. That June day on Hill 844, Howard was the foundation of all militaries, the veteran warrior who knew exactly what to do once the fighting started. Officers in command of Charlie Company were often simply too young and inexperienced. They stayed in Chu Lai and listened to Howard on the radio net. The next day Howard pinpointed through binoculars what he was sure was a North Vietnamese army headquarters. The village was a beehive of military activity. From here, the Vietnamese were staging strikes on the Marines in Chu Lai. Howard had estimated exact grid coordinates for Marine howitzers to destroy the headquarters. But an artillery barrage would tip the enemy they were under observation—likely from Marines on Hill 844. Instead, Howard located a Bird Dog, a single-engine Cessna O-1, the eyes of the jet pilots known as Fast Movers. In Vietnam, only a Bird Dog pilot could locate a target for Mach 1 Phantoms and their 500-pound bomb load. Villagers below were used to forward air controllers flying overhead. Bird Dog twisted and turned over the village as Howard guided him to the target. "What have you got, Carnival Time?" Bird Dog asked, using Howard's radio call sign. Once certain of the target, Bird Dog called for help on the Tactical Air radio network. Musket Three, a twin-engine F-4 Phantom, said he was minutes away. Bird Dog flew low and within a few feet of the target exploded a rocket of white phosphorous. "I got your smoke," radioed Musket Three, who spotted the cloud of Willie Pete. "I'm rolling in hot from the east." A long black plume of exhaust trailed the fighter-bomber as it silently pickled two 500-pound bombs exactly on the suspected headquarters. The roar of the engines came moments later, followed by many explosions that proved the enemy HQ was an arsenal for the North Vietnamese regulars. A frenzy of villagers ran toward the plume of black smoke that arose from the destruction.

Howard and his recon team had also exploded a hornet's nest. Perhaps it was the precision of the attack. Hundreds of North Vietnamese the very next night swarmed to the base of Hill 844. They banged bamboo together so that it sounded like thunder. Then every one of the attackers seemed to have a whistle. There was a brief bugle call, then shouts: "Marines, you die tonight" and "Marines, you die in one hour." Earlier in the day, Howard had waved off a headquarters suggestion that his tiny force be extracted. "We have a defensible position," he radioed. As the size of the attack unfolded, Howard realized he had been overconfident. The blackness of the night and high grass all the way up the mountain hillside hid the enemy until they were on the edge of the Marine defense and began throwing grenades. Howard moved from one fire team to another, giving instructions, redeploying some, insisting on semiautomatic fire from the M-14s. Full automatic fire would only draw concentrated replies—the enemy would think it was a machine gun. Howard had designated a box of grid coordinates in front of his troops for Marine artillery. Green tracers from the Vietnamese AK-47s streaked uphill. Red tracers from the Marine M-14s poured downhill. Howard called for flares. They lit the hillsides swarming with Vietnamese, something like turning on the kitchen light and seeing the cockroaches scurry. Then Howard adjusted artillery fire on the attackers. Still they came, firing and maneuvering, like any well-trained army. Howard turned back a Huey helicopter medevac that came to rescue the mounting number of wounded. "It would be suicide," he told the pilot. Two Huey gunships with rockets and machines raked the attackers. Around 3 a.m., a Marine A-4 Skyhawk rolled in over the battlefield that had been lit by blinding flares. The fighter-bomber dropped 250-pound bombs.

As the Vietnamese penetrated their perimeter, knife fighting ensued. Howard pulled his battered platoon into a tighter defensive position on Hill 488's knob. By 4 a.m., the air strikes had cured the Vietnamese of making new mass attacks. At dawn most retreated, except for snipers within yards of the Marines. To preserve ammunition, Howard advised throwing rocks. *Has it come to that?* Hildreth thought? Howard explained, "They will think we have their grenades. When they jump out of the way, we'll zap 'em." Hildreth assembled a pile of stones and began picking off one man after another. Howard was wounded in his testicles by grenade shrapnel. He refused morphine, saying the other wounded needed it more. Seven others were so seriously wounded that they were unconscious and could not move. Six were dead. Also killed were four Marines sent to Hill 488 during the most intense fighting. Enemy dead were estimated in the hundreds. Their bodies were removed from the battlefield before the Marines could count them.

Back in Chu Lai, once the after-action assessment was finished, Carnival Time Company Commander Timothy Geraghty and other commanders would begin the holiest of holy processes: sorting out commendations for the heroes of Hill 488. Eventually, four Navy Crosses—the second-highest award for valor—were awarded to the men of 1st Platoon. The Silver Star—third-highest—went to 14. There were also 13 Purple Hearts.

A year later in the White House, President Lyndon B. Johnson draped around the neck of Gunnery Sergeant Jimmie Earl Howard

a ribbon of sky blue with a field of white stars that held the Medal
of Honor. "Howard was largely responsible for preventing the loss
of the entire platoon," the citation said. The award would result in
invitations for Howard and Geraghty 16 years later to a sumptuous
Manhattan dinner. It was the annual convention of the Congressional Medal of Honor Society.

As an honored guest, Geraghty was on the dais at the Sheraton
Center dining room. It was December 12, 1983, barely two months
after his command was destroyed in Beirut. "I felt pretty uncomfortable there having just returned home from a tragedy and a failed
mission," Geraghty said. The Pentagon would soon absolve his superiors and blame Geraghty for the tragedy. An awkward moment
occurred before the dinner. Geraghty bumped into Defense Secretary Caspar Weinberger.

"Standing face to face we looked at each other," Geraghty said.
"I believe he recognized me. As I took a step forward to pay my respects, his face became very flushed. He suddenly looked down at
some cards he was carrying and raced off in another direction."

Ruffles and flourishes rang through the hall, followed by an endless rendition of "Hail to the Chief." The president of the United
States entered, tall and broad-shouldered in a blue suit and a red tie.
Ronald Reagan was in his element. "His presence as he entered the
room was impressive and pervading," Geraghty said.

Throughout his career, and particularly as president, Reagan attached himself to military heroics and elevated them with soaring
speeches. In his speech that night, he said nothing of the 241 dead
Marines in Beirut. The Grenada victory was another matter.

"Our forces had what they needed to get the job done," he said.
"And now the world knows that when it comes to our national
security, the United States will do whatever it takes to protect the

safety and freedom of the American people. May I just say that, as of this morning, 950 of the 82nd Airborne are enplaned on their way back to this country—the last of the combat troops in Grenada."

Then he shared his favorite World War II Medal of Honor account with the audience.

"A B-17 [was] coming back across the Channel from a raid over Europe, badly shot up by antiaircraft. The ball turret that hung underneath the belly of the plane had taken a hit," Reagan said. "The young ball-turret gunner was wounded, and they couldn't get him out of the turret there while flying.

"But over the channel, the plane began to lose altitude, and the commander had to order bail out. And as the men started to leave the plane, the last one to leave—the boy, understandably, knowing he was left behind to go down with the plane, cried out in terror—the last man to leave the plane saw the commander sit down on the floor. He took the boy's hand and said, 'Never mind, son, we'll ride it down together.' Congressional Medal of Honor, posthumously awarded."

The story was untrue. A colleague of mine went through 436 Medal of Honor citations for the period and found nothing to match the account that Reagan had told many times. Something like that story was in a *Reader's Digest* article that Reagan might have read. My colleague traced it back to a *New York Herald Tribune* reporter who said he heard it at a bomber base during the war. Nothing solid, of course.

Like everyone else, the audience that night liked a good story that left a lump in the throat. Applause echoed through the hall. Afterward, Reagan stood in a brief informal receiving line for the distinguished guests, who included Marine Colonel Timothy Geraghty. He came face to face with Silver Screen Six.

"The president told me how proud our nation was of the courage, discipline, and sacrifice of the Marines in Beirut," Geraghty said. "He was very gracious." The words bonded Geraghty to Reagan for the rest of his life. Geraghty would have only uncritical words for his commander in chief.

"On behalf of the Marine Corps, I thanked him for his kind words and simply said, 'Semper Fi, Mr. President.'"

ACKNOWLEDGMENTS

As a young police reporter on the dawn beat for *The Baltimore News-Post,* I pulled up to a roadhouse in East Baltimore where there was a report of murder. I had seen enough dead that I was not anxious to go inside. The detectives had left. Out of the joint in a rush came Toby Joyce, pink, white hair in a crew cut, one eye always looking to one side. He was the police reporter for an all-news radio station. He walked over, opened his notebook, and gave me every fact about the crime. I need not go inside nor seek the cops. It was my first "fill" as a journalist. Someday, I might return the favor when Toby arrived late on the scene. In future, I always tried to maintain the tradition by sharing what my shoe leather produced. For this book, I got a number of "fills" from fellow journalists.

Abraham Rabinovich, a colleague, a reporter for *The Jerusalem Post* and the author of the definitive *The Yom Kippur War: The Epic Encounter That Transformed the Middle East,* sharpened my facts about a desert war that I got secondhand while covering the Nixon White House.

David Blundy of *The London Sunday Times,* Martin Woollacott of *The Guardian,* and Patrick Cockburn of the *Financial Times* kept me from losing my way on treacherous byroads in the Mideast. While I was a 21-year veteran of Washington journalism in 1981, I was a rookie when it came to the state of play in Israel, Lebanon, and Syria. They gave me the road map.

Ze'ev Schiff, the military correspondent for the Israeli daily newspaper *Haaretz,* was without equal when it came to unearthing the deepest secrets of the Jerusalem government. His book with Ehud Ya'ari, *Israel's Lebanon War,* details almost every machination between Prime Minister Menachem Begin, Defense Minister Ariel Sharon, and the nefarious Christians of Lebanon. Ze'ev was relentless, accurate, fair, and endlessly patient with my questions.

David Martin of CBS gleaned every detail from the Department of Defense as a reward for the shoe leather expended on unforgiving concrete rings of the Puzzle Palace. Showing up daily, Martin dominated the Pentagon with incisive coverage as almost every general and service secretary angled for prime time. His book *Best Laid Plans: The Inside Story of America's War Against Terrorism,* written with another friend, John Walcott, shows a mastery of classified information and vital interviews.

John Boykin, whom I never met, did the best job of journaling the ups and down of Philip Habib, Reagan's Mideast troubleshooter. Boykin's book *Cursed Is the Peacemaker* showed the fragility of American influence in Jerusalem and Damascus during 1982 and 1983.

Marine Colonel Timothy Geraghty waited nine years to tell his side of events in Beirut. His book *Peacekeepers at War* has an ironic title that spotlights the conflicting mission that led to the 1983 massacre of his command. It offers insights and details that go to the heart of Ronald Reagan's bungled policies.

Jennifer Mandel, a National Archives researcher at Ronald Reagan's Presidential Library, was very helpful in wading through the files in Simi Valley, California. Samantha Zukergood, my editor at St. Martin's, and Brooke Kroeger, kept things clean.

NOTES

RRPLM: Ronald Reagan Presidential Library and Museum, Simi Valley, California, www.reaganlibrary.gov.

1. Four Inches

Note to readers: As a Washington reporter in 1973, I reported on the Arab-Israeli War from the Defense and State Departments and the White House. Many of the facts in this chapter come from firsthand reporting on these issues.

"Just to see . . ." Kissinger, Anwar Sadat Lecture for Peace, University of Maryland, May 4, 2000.

"We continue to . . ." Combined Watch Report of the US Intelligence Board, Oct. 4, 1973, in *President Nixon and the Role of Intelligence in the 1973 Arab-Israeli War* (Yorba Linda, CA: RRPLM, 2013), 45.

"Both the Israelis and the Arabs . . ." Central Intelligence Bulletin, Oct. 6, 1973, in ibid.

'Listen, I'm of Jewish origin . . .' Kissinger, Anwar Sadat Lecture for Peace, University of Maryland, May 4, 2000.

"Who in the hell . . ." Dino Brugioni, "The Effects of Aerial and Satellite Imagery on the 1973 Yom Kippur War," *Air Power History,* vol. 51, no. 3 (Fall 2004), 4–13.

"If we could recapture . . ." Sadat, *In Search of Identity,* 244.

"A statesman has to take . . ." and "I don't know any expert . . ." Kissinger, Anwar Sadat Lecture for Peace, University of Maryland, May 4, 2000.

"I don't know . . ." Minutes of the Secretary of State's Staff Meeting, Oct. 26, 1973, doc. 229, *Foreign Relations of the United States, 1969–1976,* vol. 26, *Energy Crisis, 1969–1974.*

"Our difficulty was partly . . ." Doc. 63, "The October War and U.S. Policy," National Security Archive, Oct. 7, 2003, https://nsarchive2.gwu.edu/NSAEBB/NSAEBB98/.

"Item one," Sadat said," Finklestone, *Anwar Sadat,* 36.

"What's all this nonsense . . ." William Joseph Burns, *Economic Aid and American Policy toward Egypt, 1955–1981* (Albany: 1984, State University of New York Press), l66.

"This allows you to have . . ." Documentary, "Battle Stations—SR-71 Blackbird Stealth Plane." https://vodeocatalog.com/ru/video/YJ5FjVOvkB0.

"Most of the fortified positions," Brugioni, "The Effects of Aerial and Satellite Imagery," 8–9.

"It was a generation that had never lost . . ." Simon Dunstan, *The Yom Kippur War 1973 (2): The Sinai* (Oxford: Osprey, 2003, 2008), 53.

"As events turned grim . . ." Adam Raz, "The Significance of the Reputed Yom Kippur War Nuclear Affair," *Strategic Affairs* 16, no. 4 (2014), 103–18.

"Hersh had the . . ." Hersh, *The Samson Option,* 245.

"We did know around this time . . ." William Quandt, *Washington Post,* Oct. 24, 1991.

"When I talked . . ." Phone conversation between Gen. Brent Scowcroft and Kissinger, Oct. 11, 1973, Foreign Relations of the United States.

"Schlesinger had his own . . ." Haig, *Inner Circles,* 131.

"you can make war with Soviet arms . . ." Kissinger, Anwar Sadat Lecture for Peace, University of Maryland, May 4, 2000.

"It is ridiculous . . ." Memorandum of Conversation, Nov. 29, 1973, doc. 251, ibid.

"He had tears in his eyes . . ." Kissinger, Anwar Sadat Lecture for Peace, University of Maryland, May 4, 2000.

"This allows you . . ." *Battle Stations,* History Channel documentary, Dec. 15, 2000.

2. Legacy

Note to readers: As a reporter, I covered the assassination of Sadat and his burial. All of the material in this chapter is based on interviews and eyewitness accounts.

3. A Vain Fantasy

"A Jewish-Christian front . . ." and "A vain fantasy . . ." Schiff and Ya'ari, *Israel's Lebanon War,* 13–14.

"Our guiding principle . . ." Ibid., 18.

"Bashir, when he wasn't . . ." Crist, *Twilight War,* 113.

"Like a lobotomy . . ." Boykin, *Cursed Is the Peacemaker,* 55–57.

"We do not intend to attack . . ." Schiff and Ya'ari, *Israel's Lebanon War,* 73.

"Our aim is not to see . . .", 55.

"The thing about the Israelis . . ." Boykin, *Cursed Is the Peacemaker,* 56.

"The president signed . . ." Bob Woodward, "Alliance with a Lebanese Leader," *Washington Post,* Sept. 29, 1987.

4. Mole Cricket

"They're all PLO . . ." Schiff and Ya'ari, *Israel's Lebanon War,* 98.

"I am astounded . . ." Boykin, *Cursed Is the Peacemaker,* 65.

5. The Siege

"In one case, on August 6, . . ." Jonathan Randall, "Israel Launches New Attacks as Talks Advance," *Washington Post,* Aug. 7, 1982, A1, and "200 Killed as Israelis Step Up Beirut Raids," *Irish Times,* Aug. 7, 1982, 1.

"We are now dealing . . ." John Corry, "TV: View of NBC Coverage of Lebanon Invasion," *New York Times,* Feb. 18, 1984.

"There wasn't any heavy . . ." Boykin, *Cursed Is the Peacemaker,* 85.

"Philip hated . . ." Ibid., 46.

"Habib didn't like . . ." Ibid., 88.

"didn't know his ass from third base . . ." Boykin, *One Brief Miracle,* chapter 2.

"He wasn't a mean man . . ." William Clark interview cited in Reeves, *President Reagan: The Triumph of Imagination,* 111.

"Hold out for . . ." Schiff and Ya'ari, *Israel's Lebanon War,* 202.

"I was pretty blunt . . ." R. Reagan, *The Reagan Diaries,* 89.

"Actually, the only . . ." Ibid., 91.

"was begging me to do something . . ." Ibid., 98.

"He hurt me very deeply . . ." John Kifner, interview, 2014.

6. Turmoil

"The President has noted . . ." "Statement by Deputy Press Secretary Speakes on the Presidential Election in Lebanon," Aug. 23, 1982, *Public Papers,* RRPLM.

"Where do we stand . . ." Schiff and Ya'ari, *Israel's Lebanon War,* 234.

"When the French government sent . . ." Hammel, *The Root,* 28.

"The Jewish public's . . ." Commission of Inquiry into the Events at the Refugee Camps in Beirut, "Report of the Commission," Feb. 8, 1983. All further related quotes come from this document.

"I don't want a single one of them left . . ." Schiff and Ya'ari, *Israel's Lebanon War,* 255.

"Circumstances changed . . ." Ibid., 259.

"Something snapped . . ." Ibid., 280.

"Before their eyes . . ." Shlaim, *The Iron Wall,* 107.

7. Going for Broke

"The wholly righteous . . ." "Message on the Observance of the Jewish High Holy Days," Sept. 17, 1982, *Public Papers,* RRPLM.

"It is true . . ." "Remarks in White House Station, New Jersey, on the Situation in Lebanon," Sept. 17, 1982, *Public Papers,* RRPLM.

"In Beirut, Haddad's . . ." and "The Israelis did finally attempt . . ." R. Reagan, *Reagan Diaries,* 101.

"I ask Italy . . ." Henry Kanm, "Arafat Demands 3 Nations Return Peace Force to Beirut," *New York Times,* Sept. 17, 1982.

"The guilt feeling . . ." and "I don't think . . ." Martin and Walcott, *Best Laid Plans,* 95–96.

"The Italian force was . . ." Cannon, *President Reagan,* 356.

"Sharon was a killer . . ." Boykin, *Cursed Is the Peacemaker,* 271.

"when the Palestinian fighters . . ." "The President's News Conference,"
Sept. 28, 1982, *Public Papers,* RRPLM.

"I finally told our group . . ." R. Reagan, *Reagan Diaries,* 101.

"There were those of us . . ." Martin and Walcott, *Best Laid Plans,* 97.

"Mr. President, do you have a plan . . ." "The President's News Conference,"
Sept. 28, 1982, *Public Papers,* RRPLM. https://www.reaganlibrary.gov
/research/speeches/92882c.

"George Shultz, God bless his soul . . ." Boykin, *Cursed Is the Peace-maker,* 103.

8. A Path to Glory

"I worked 85 hours . . ." McFarlane, *Special Trust,* 80.

"Look, you're going to be . . ." Timberg, *The Nightingale's Song,* 57.

"Graham, you have . . ." Ibid., 219.

"There's McFarlane . . ." Richard Allen Oral History, May 28, 2002,
Miller Center, University of Virginia, Charlottesville.

"But you do . . ." McFarlane, *Special Trust,* 193–94.

"It has five components . . ." McFarlane, Ibid.

"He was able . . ." Bernard Weinraub, "Habib's Right-hand Man," *New
York Times,* Sept. 9, 1982.

"You know, Bud . . ." Timberg, *The Nightingale's Song,* 323.

9. The Party of God

"Dodge's release was . . ." Interview with George Shultz.

"All of a sudden, . . ." Interview with Ambassador Robert S. Dillon,
May 17, 1990, Association for Diplomatic Studies and Training, For-eign Affairs Oral History Project.

"Although it was . . ." Martin and Walcott, *Best Laid Plans,* 108.

"More applicable . . ." Ibid., 10.

10. Peace in a Madhouse

"Sir, you have to . . ." Geraghty, *Peacekeepers at War,* 62.

"Who is that? . . ." Ibid., 62.

"He had enlisted . . ." "Military Service of Ronald Reagan," RRPLM website.

"I'm sure you are aware . . ." "Rare Recording of Reagan-Begin Conversation Released," *Haaretz,* Nov. 10, 2014.

"Some Democrats . . ." Stuart Taylor Jr., "Questions Raised Again on Reagan's Limits Under War Powers Act," *New York Times,* Oct. 24, 1983.

"I'm up on job rating . . ." R. Reagan, *The Reagan Diaries,* 184.

"Not easy. . . ." Ibid., 177.

"We needed to stand . . ." Shultz, *Turmoil and Triumph,* 226.

"I can't get the idea . . ." R. Reagan, *The Reagan Diaries,* 177.

"The president expressed . . ." Geraghty, *Peacekeepers at War,* 62.

"Doing Israel's dirty work . . ." "Valor Without Glamor in Lebanon," *New York Times,* Aug. 30, 1983.

11. Moment of Truth

"NSC sons-of-bitches . . ." Interview with Ambassador Robert S. Dillon, May 17, 1990, Association for Diplomatic Studies and Training, Foreign Affairs Oral History Project; cited below as Dillon interview, FAOHP.

"I immediately protested . . ." McFarlane, *Special Trust,* 250.

"I could have lived . . ." Dillon interview, FAOHP.

"They didn't trust him . . ." Ibid.

"they believed they had a duty . . ." Ibid.

"There is a serious . . ." McFarlane, *Special Trust,* 250.

"My multiple intelligence sources . . ." Geraghty, *Peacekeepers at War,* 56.

"It was time . . ." Reeves, *President Reagan,* 172.

"Let me set the record straight . . ." "Interview with Bruce Drake of the
    New York Daily News," Dec. 12, 1983, *Public Papers,* RRPLM.

"It has been determined . . ." NSDD 103, "National Security Decision Di-
    rectives," RRPLM website, https://www.reaganlibrary.gov/digital-library
    /nsdds.

"The Joint Chiefs relayed . . ." Geraghty, *Peacekeepers at War,* 64–65.

"It would mark . . ." Ibid., 65.

"What followed was a rancorous week . . ." Ibid.

"I yelled . . ." and "Sir, I can't . . ." Ibid.

"I refused the air strike mission . . ." Ibid., 67.

"The stakes continued to be raised . . ." Ibid., 69.

"There was no reason . . ." Ibid., 72.

"Nevertheless, the situation . . ." McFarlane, *Special Trust,* 252.

"It was another occasion . . ." Geraghty, *Peacekeepers at War,* 72.

12. Burying the Marines

"His eyes opened wide . . ." Geraghty, *Peacekeepers at War,* 108.

"Again, Mitterrand and his party . . ." Ibid.

"I begged the President . . ." Caspar Weinberger Oral History, Nov. 19,
    2002, Miller Center, University of Virginia, Charlottesville.

"I know there are no words . . ." "Remarks to Reporters on the Death
    of American and French Military Personnel in Beirut, Lebanon,"
    Oct. 23, 1983, *Public Papers,* RRPLM.

"You are going to eat . . ." Geraghty, *Peacekeepers at War,* 117.

"Hit the deck . . ." Report of the Department of Defense Commission on Beirut International Airport Terrorist Act, Oct. 23, 1983.

"He went next door . . ." Howard Baker Oral History, Aug. 24, 2004, Miller Center, University of Virginia, Charlottesville.

"Despite what the administration claimed . . ." "The Speaker Speaks Out," *Chicago Tribune,* Sept. 13, 1987.

"What reports have you received . . ." "Remarks of the President and Prime Minister Eugenia Charles of Dominica Announcing the Deployment of United States Forces in Grenada," Oct. 25, 1983, *Public Papers,* RRPLM.

"to take spectacular . . ." Ibid., 172.

"Mr. President, when I was . . ." "The President's News Conference," Oct. 19, 1983, *Public Papers,* RRPLM.

"As I surveyed . . ." Ibid., 100.

"both proposals were rejected . . ." Shultz, *Turmoil and Triumph,* 326.

"His orders enabled . . ." US Army Center of Military History Department, Operation Urgent Fury, July 15, 2004.

"The events in Lebanon and Grenada . . ." "Address to the Nation on Events in Lebanon and Grenada," Oct. 27, 1983, *Public Papers,* RRPLM.

"The speech must have . . ." R. Reagan, *The Reagan Diaries,* 191.

"I came here today . . ." "Remarks to Military Personnel at Cherry Point, North Carolina, on the United States Casualties in Lebanon and Grenada, Nov. 4, 1983, *Public Papers,* RRPLM.

"I do not believe . . ." "Remarks and a Question-and-Answer Session with Reporters on the Pentagon Report on the Security of United States Marines in Lebanon," Dec. 27, 1983, *Public Papers,* RRPLM.

"Although this letter . . ." Geraghty, *Peacekeepers at War,* 163.

13. Path to Iran

"Debbie, our worst . . ." *Deborah D. Peterson for the estate of James C. Knipple, plaintiffs, v. The Islamic Republic of Iran, et al., defendants,* US District Court for the District of Columbia, transcript, 20.

"We have strong circumstantial evidence . . ." "Address to the Nation on Events in Lebanon and Grenada," Oct. 27, 1983, *Public Papers,* RRPLM.

"I guess there's three words . . ." "Procedure," *American International Law Cases,* Fourth Series, vol. 4, 2009, 1473 (New York: Oceana, Oxford University Press).

"We're not going . . ." Reagan phone call to Mitterrand, Oct. 24, 1983, Box 17, National Security Files, #7664, RRPLM.

"The approval of . . ." Allen Lengel, "Judge: Iran Behind '83 Beirut Bombing Allows Families of U.S. Troops to Collect Damages," *Washington Post,* May 31, 2003, 8.

"You don't have to go any further . . ." "Radio Address to the Nation on Proposed Natural Gas Deregulation Legislation," Feb. 26, 1983, *Public Papers,* RRPLM.

"The President gave his approval . . ." McFarlane, *Special Trust,* 270.

"It is beneath our dignity . . ." Micah Zenko, "When Reagan Cut and Run," *Foreign Policy,* Feb. 7, 2014.

"We cannot opt out . . ." Bernard Gwertzman, "Shultz Supports Armed Reprisals," *New York Times,* Jan. 16, 1986.

"Yes, the situation . . ." "Radio Address to the Nation on the Budget Deficit, Central America, and Lebanon," Feb. 4, 1984, *Public Papers,* RRPLM.

"You have any good friends? . . ." Thomas L. Friedman, "Marines Complete Beirut Pullback," *New York Times,* Feb. 27, 1984.

"Let's have . . ." Thomas L. Friedman, "U.S. Combat Units Begin Pulling Out of Beirut Bunkers," *New York Times,* Feb. 26, 1984.

"You see that surf, . . ." Friedman, "Marines Complete."

"What's the plan? . . ." "Informal Exchange with Reporters on the Trans World Airlines Hijacking Incident," June 23, 1985, *Public Papers,* RRPLM.

"Jimmy Reagan . . ." Review & Outlook (editorial), *Wall Street Journal,* June 20, 1985, 1.

"What was to be . . ." Martin and Walcott, *Best Laid Plans,* 202.

14. End of an Era

"He liked to leave them . . ." Caspar Weinberger Oral History, Nov. 19, 2002, Miller Center, University of Virginia, Charlottesville.

"Doesn't it make you angry . . ." Myra McPherson, "The Final Days: The Sound and the Flurry," *Washington Post,* Nov. 4, 1980.

"In Chicago . . ." As quoted in Josh Levin, "The Welfare Queen," *Slate .com,* Dec. 19, 2013.

"We somehow laugh . . ." Robert Provine, "The Science of Laughter," *Psychology Today,* Nov. 1, 2000.

"The popularity of Ronald Reagan . . ." Deaver, *Behind the Scenes,* 23.

"Many people were shocked . . ." Tip O'Neill and William Novak, "Tip: 'Reagan Was the Worst' Former House Speaker Tip O'Neill Calls the President Amiable but Short on Details." (Excerpt from O'Neill, *Man of the House*) *Sun-Sentinel,* Sept. 13, 1987. https://www.sun-sentinel .com/news/fl-xpm-1987-09-13-8703130479-story.html.

"For their second debate . . ." Quotations from the debate in the following pages are from the transcript, "Debate Between the President and Former Vice President Walter F. Mondale in Kansas City, Missouri," Oct. 21, 1984, *Public Papers,* RRPLM.

"He does what he has to do . . ." Mary McGrory, "Two Eye-opening En- counters," *Washington Post,* Oct. 25, 1984.

"He delivered the perfect . . ." David Broder, "Encounter Leaves Reagan on Course," *Washington Post,* Oct. 22, 1984.

"It was just hilarious . . ." Max Friedersdorf Oral History, Oct. 24, 2002, Miller Center, University of Virginia, Charlottesville.

"I was shocked . . ." O'Neill and Novak, "Tip: 'Reagan Was the Worst . . .'" *Sun-Sentinel,* from O'Neill, *Man of the House,* Sept. 13, 1987, https://www.sun-sentinel.com/news/fl-xpm-1987-09-13-8703130479-story.html.

"I could have been speaking Latin . . ." Ibid.

"Reagan continued to soar . . ." "Ronald Reagan from the People's Perspective," Gallup, June 7, 2004, https://news.gallup.com/poll/11887/ronald-reagan-from-peoples-perspective-gallup-poll-review.aspx.

"You're going to hear the facts . . ." "Address to the Nation on the Iran Arms and Contra Aid Controversy," Nov. 13, 1986, *Public Papers,* RRPLM.

"What would be wrong . . ." "The President's News Conference," Nov. 19, 1986, *Public Papers,* RRPLM.

"The president was unmoved . . ." Shultz, *Turmoil and Triumph,* 838.

"Henry came back from the Oval Office . . ." Alexander Haig Oral History, Nov. 30, 2007, Richard Nixon Presidential Library and Museum, Yorba Linda, California.

"Galatians 3:8 . . ." "White House Verifies Reagan Did Write in Bible Sent to Iran," *Los Angeles Times,* Jan. 30, 1987.

"A few months ago . . ." "Address to the Nation on the Iran Arms and Contra Aid Controversy," March 4, 1987, *Public Papers,* RRPLM.

"He welcomed to the White House . . ." "Remarks Congratulating the Championship University of Notre Dame Football Team, Jan. 18, 1989, *Public Papers,* RRPLM. https://www.presidency.ucsb.edu/documents/remarks-congratulating-the-championship-university-notre-dame-football-team.

"Knute liked . . ." "Remarks at a Senate Campaign Fundraising Reception for Pete Dawkins of New Jersey," Apr. 19, 1988, *Public Papers*, RRPLM.

Epilogue

"*Enchanting*, Hildreth thought . . ." Hildreth and Barber, *Hill 488*, 161.

"The men like him . . ." Ibid., 136.

"Howard advised throwing rocks. . . ." Ibid., 279.

"I felt pretty uncomfortable . . ." Geraghty, *Peacekeepers at War*, 176.

"Standing face to face . . ." Ibid.

"Our forces had what they needed . . ." "Remarks at the Annual Convention of the Congressional Medal of Honor Society in New York City," Dec. 12, 1983, *Public Papers*, RRPLM.

"The president told me . . ." Geraghty, *Peacekeepers at War*, 176.

BIBLIOGRAPHY

Baer, Robert. *See No Evil: The True Story of a Ground Soldier in the CIA's War on Terrorism.* New York: Three Rivers Press, 2002.

Ball, George W. *Error and Betrayal in Lebanon: An Analysis of Israel's Invasion of Lebanon and the Implications for US–Israeli Relations.* Washington, DC: Foundation for Middle East Peace, 1984.

Boykin, John. *Cursed Is the Peacemaker: The American Diplomat Versus the Israeli General, Beirut 1982.* Belmont, CA: Applegate Press, 2002.

———. *One Brief Miracle: the Diplomat, the Zealot, and the Wild Blundering Siege.* Bookbaby, 2014.

Brands, H. W. *Reagan: The Life.* New York: Doubleday, 2015.

Cannon, Lou. *President Reagan: The Role of a Lifetime.* New York: Simon & Schuster, 1991.

Carter, Jimmy. *The Blood of Abraham: Insights into the Middle East.* Fayetteville: University of Arkansas Press, 2007.

———. *White House Diary.* New York: Farrar, Straus & Giroux, 2010.

Clarke, Richard A. *Against All Enemies: Inside America's War on Terror.* New York: Free Press, 2004.

Commission of Inquiry into the Events at the Refugee Camps in Beirut. "Report of the Commission," February 8, 1983. https://mfa.gov

.il/mfa/foreignpolicy/mfadocuments/yearbook6/pages/104%20report
%20of%20the%20commission%20of%20inquiry%20into%20the
%20e.aspx (accessed January 25, 2019).

Crist, David. *The Twilight War: The Secret History of America's Thirty-Year Conflict with Iran.* New York: Penguin, 2013.

Deaver, Michael K., with Mickey Herskowitz. *Behind the Scenes.* New York: William Morrow, 1987.

Doran, Michael. *Ike's Gamble: America's Rise to Dominance in the Middle East.* New York: Free Press, 2016.

Finklestone, Joseph. *Anwar Sadat: Visionary Who Dared.* London: Routledge, 2013.

Geraghty, Timothy J., USMC (Ret.) *Peacekeepers at War: Beirut 1983—The Marine Commander Tells His Story.* Washington, DC: Potomac Books, 2009.

Gordon, Matthew S. *The Gemayels: World Leaders Past and Present.* New York: Chelsea House, 1988.

Haig, Alexander M., Jr. *Caveat: Realism, Reagan, and Foreign Policy.* New York: Macmillan, 1984.

Haig, Alexander M. Jr., with Charles McCarry. *Inner Circles: How America Changed the World: A Memoir.* New York: Warner, 1992.

Hammel, Eric. *The Root: The Marines in Beirut, August 1982–February 1984.* Pacifica, CA: Pacifica Press, 1985.

Hersh, Seymour M. *The Samson Option: Israel's Nuclear Arsenal and American Foreign Policy.* New York: Random House, 1991.

Hildreth, Ray, and Charles W. Sasser. *Hill 488.* New York: Pocket Books, 2003.

Hirst, David. *Beware of Small States: Lebanon, Battleground of the Middle East.* New York: Nation Books, 2010.

Kornbluh, Peter, and Malcolm Byrne, eds. *The Iran-Contra Scandal: The*

Declassified History. National Security Archives Documents Reader series. New York: New Press, 1993.

Martin, David C., and John Walcott. *Best Laid Plans.* New York: Harper & Row, 1988.

Matthews, Chris. *Tip and the Gipper: When Politics Worked.* New York: Simon & Schuster, 2013.

McFarlane, Robert C., with Zofia Smardz. *Special Trust.* New York: Cadell & Davies, 1994.

Morris, Roger. *Haig: The General's Progress.* New York: Playboy Press, 1982.

Nofziger, Lyn. *Nofziger.* Washington, DC: Regnery Gateway, 1992.

O'Neill, Tip, with William Novak. *Man of the House: The Life and Political Memoirs of Speaker Tip O'Neill.* New York: Random House, 1987.

Rabinovich, Abraham. *The Yom Kippur War: The Epic Encounter That Transformed the Middle East.* New York: Schocken Books, 2004.

Rabinovich, Itamar. *The War for Lebanon, 1970–1985.* Ithaca, NY: Cornell University Press, 1984.

Reagan, Nancy, with William Novak. *My Turn: The Memoirs of Nancy Reagan.* New York: Random House, 1989.

Reagan, Ronald. *The Reagan Diaries.* Edited by Douglas Brinkley. New York: HarperCollins, 2007.

Reeves, Richard. *President Reagan: The Triumph of Imagination.* New York: Simon & Schuster, 2005.

Sadat, Anwar. *In Search of Identity: An Autobiography.* New York: Harper & Row, 1978.

Schiff, Ze'ev, and Ehud Ya'ari. *Israel's Lebanon War.* New York: Simon & Schuster, 1984.

Seale, Patrick, with Maureen McConville. *Asad: The Struggle for the Middle East.* Berkeley: University of California Press, 1988.

Shlaim, Avi. *The Iron Wall: Israel and the Arab World*. Updated and expanded ed. New York: W. W. Norton, 2014.

Shultz, George P. *Turmoil and Triumph: My Years as Secretary of State*. New York: Charles Scribner's Sons, 1993.

Timberg, Robert. *The Nightingale's Song*. New York: Simon & Schuster, 1995.

Tyler, Patrick. *Fortress Israel*. New York: Farrar, Straus & Giroux, 2012.

Wapshott, Nicholas. *Ronald Reagan and Margaret Thatcher: A Political Marriage*. New York: Penguin Group, 2007.

Weinberger, Caspar W., with Gretchen Roberts. *In the Arena: A Memoir of the 20th Century*. Washington, DC: Regnery, 2001.

Wilson, George C. *Supercarrier: An Inside Account of Life Aboard the World's Most Powerful Ship, the USS John F. Kennedy*. New York: Macmillan, 1986.

Yoshitani, Gail E. S. *Reagan on War: A Reappraisal of the Weinberger Doctrine*. College Station: Texas A&M University Press, 2012

INDEX